English network

Tourist

Lynda Hübner und Alan Seaton

Ernst Klett Sprachen

Stuttgart

English Network Tourist

Autoren:
Lynda Hübner, München
Alan Seaton, Newcastle-upon-Tyne

Beratung:
Dr. Philip Devlin, Berlin

Beratende Mitwirkung:
Janice Probert, Düsseldorf

Lehrwerkskomponenten:	
Kursbuch mit *Pocket Tourist*	606555
Audio-CD	606595
Teacher's Book	online
Lehrwerksbegleitend:	
Activity Book	606569
Pocket Grammar A1/A2	606570
Pocket Reader	606568
Pocket Short Stories	606572
Pocket Vocabulary	606573
Pocket Get in Touch	606574
Pocket America	606577

Verlagsredaktion:
Claudia Schwarz

Grafik und Layout:
Beate Andler, Projektleitung
Sabine Wittmann, München
kaltner verlagsmedien GmbH, Bobingen

Location photography:
Hermann Dörre, München

Illustrations:
Graham Round (Linda Rogers Ass.)
Jürgen Bartz
Fran Jordan

www.klett-sprachen.de/englishnetwork

1. Auflage 1 7 6 5 | 2019 18 17

Erstausgabe erschienen 2003 bei der Langenscheidt KG, München

Druck und Bindung: Elanders GmbH, Waiblingen

ISBN 978-3-12-606555-9

Welcome to *English Network Tourist*

Sie möchten im englischsprachigen Ausland Urlaub machen oder in ein Land fahren, in dem Sie sich mit Englisch verständigen können? Dann haben Sie mit *English Network Tourist* den richtigen Kurs gewählt! Mit diesem Kursbuch können Sie Ihre Englischkenntnisse vor dem Urlaub gezielt und systematisch verbessern: Sie lernen anhand von praxisnahen Situationen, die Ihnen als Tourist im Ausland begegnen, und erfahren gleichzeitig viel Neues über beliebte Urlaubsländer.

Wohin geht die Reise mit English Network Tourist?

Zunächst begleiten Sie Liz und Rolf nach Schottland. Anschließend reisen Sie mit deren Tochter Katy und Freund Sam weiter nach Australien, um schließlich einen Stopover in Hong Kong zu geniessen.
In den *Highlights* geben wir Ihnen zusätzlich interessante touristisch relevante Informationen zu den USA, Südafrika und Jamaika.

Wie ist English Network Tourist aufgebaut?

English Network Tourist ist in 12 Units gegliedert. Jede Unit besteht aus einer Doppelseite, die Sie im Kurs behandeln und einer zweiten Doppelseite, die Sie flexibel im Kurs oder zu Hause durcharbeiten können. Auf der ersten Doppelseite wird Ihnen das neue Sprachmaterial präsentiert, das Sie mit abwechslungsreichen *Activities* einüben und festigen. Die zweite Doppelseite ist zum Selbststudium vorgesehen und gibt Ihnen darüber hinaus praktische Tipps über das jeweilige Land und für Sie persönlich als Tourist im englischsprachigen Ausland.

Die *Highlights* über die Länder USA, Südafrika und die Karibikinsel Jamaika können in den Unterricht integriert werden oder auch einfach nur für Sie selbst zum unterhaltsamen und informativen Lesen dienen.

Die Comicfiguren Ivor Problem und Annie Mergency zeigen Ihnen nach je vier Units, wie Sie sich im Englischen sprachlich behelfen können, wenn im Urlaub etwas schief geht.

Mit welchen Begleitmaterialien können Sie zusätzlich arbeiten?

Zusammen mit dem Kursbuch erhalten Sie das Begleitheft *Pocket Tourist*, das ausgehend vom Kursbuch umfangreichen Wortschatz enthält, der nach Themengebieten geordnet ist. Zusätzlich können Sie hier – parallel zu den Units des Kursbuches – nochmals die neuen grammatischen Strukturen einüben und vertiefen. Aufgrund seines handlichen Formats können Sie *Pocket Tourist* auch auf Ihren Reisen mitnehmen, um am Urlaubsort schnell und problemlos nachzuschlagen.
Außerdem gibt es begleitend zum Kursbuch eine Audio-CD, auf der Sie die Dialoge der Units und die Listening-Übungen aus Unit und Selfstudy finden.

Wir wünschen Ihnen nun viel Freude beim Englischlernen und einen schönen Urlaub.

Lynda Hübner
und der Verlag

Alan Seaton

INHALT
TOURIST

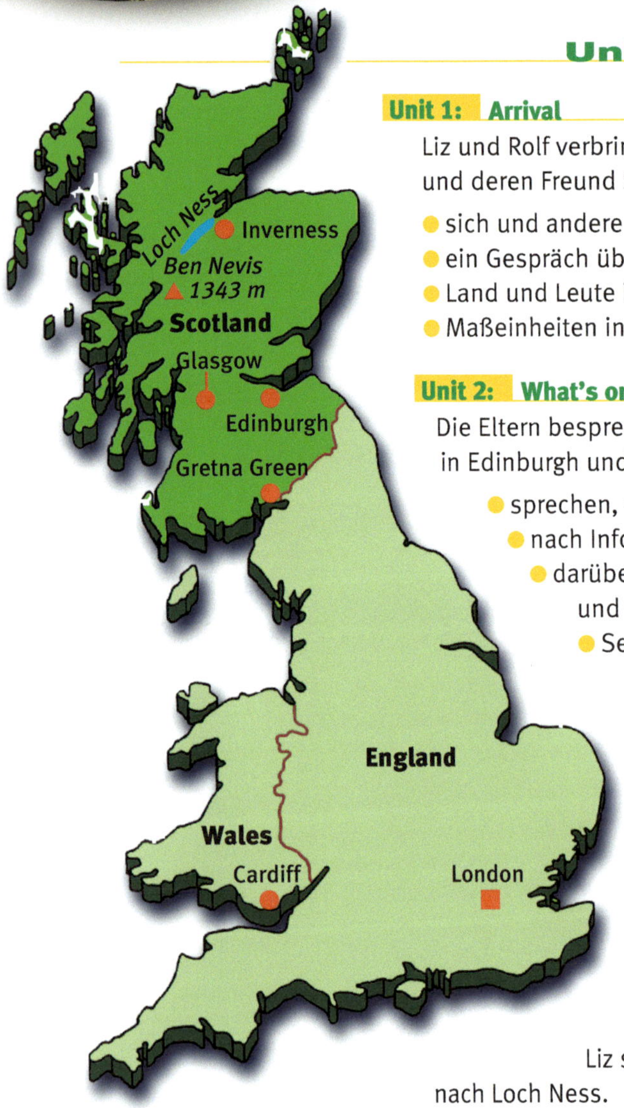

Darwin
Northern Territory
Queensland
Western Australia
Ayers Rock
867 m
Brisbane
South Australia
New South Wales
Sydney
Canberra
Perth
Victoria
Adelaide
Melbourne
Tasmania

INHALT

TOURIST

Weitere Übungen zum Unitteil:

Anhang:

Symbole:

Texte und Übungen mit diesem Symbol finden Sie auf der CD.
Die Ziffern beziehen sich auf die Spurnummern der CD: **25**

Auf der angegebenen Seite finden Sie die Lösung für die entsprechende Übung.

INTRODUCTION

This is Katy with her parents and her boyfriend, Sam. Katy was born in Stuttgart and she was brought up bi-lingually by her English mother Liz, and her German father Rolf.

Stuttgart

Edinburgh

Katy's a language student at Heriot-Watt University, Edinburgh – she wants to be an interpreter, like her mother. She shares a flat with her English boyfriend Sam Grainger, who's a radiologist at a local hospital.

Liz and Rolf are arriving for a holiday in Scotland tomorrow. They're all going to spend a few days together before Katy and Sam leave for a trip to Australia and a holiday in Hong Kong.

Sydney

WELCOME TO SCOTLAND

Katy's parents, Liz and Rolf, arrive in Edinburgh and Katy is at the airport to welcome them. They go to Katy's flat and meet her boyfriend, Sam.

Katy and Sam are going away for four weeks so Liz and Rolf can stay in the flat and spend their summer holidays in Scotland. But first the four of them enjoy some of the tourist attractions in and around Edinburgh.

Scottish islands

A Scottish pub

Princes Street, Edinburgh

UNIT 1
ARRIVAL

Niagara Falls, Canada

Taj Mahal, India

1 Starter

Introduce yourself to the person next to you:
Hello, my name's (Nicola) and I'm from (Munich).
I'm in this course because I want to travel to (Canada).

Then introduce your partner to the rest of the class: *This is (Peter) and he's from (Linz). He's in this class because he wants to travel to (India).*

Remember: *I want* but *He / She / It wants.*

2 2 Welcome

Liz: Look! There's Katy.
Rolf: Where? I can't see her.
Liz: Over there, near the cash dispensers.
Katy: Mum, Dad, wonderful to see you!
Liz: Katy, dear. How are you?
Katy: I'm fine, thanks, Mum.
Dad, lovely to see you.
Rolf: Hello, Katy.
Katy: Give me your bag, Mum.
Liz: No, it's okay. It isn't heavy.
Rolf: These cases are heavy!
Liz: Well, we can put the luggage on a trolley. Now, where are the taxis?
Katy: We don't need a taxi, Mum.
The car's in the car park.
Rolf: What? Do you have a car, Katy?
Katy: No, but Sam has a car.
Rolf: Ah, yes ... the boyfriend!
Liz: We're looking forward to meeting him.

3 Say it another way

Find words in the text which have a similar meaning to the underlined words.

1 Near the cash machines.
2 Great to see you. (2x)
3 I'm very well.
4 Hi, Katy
5 It's all right.
6 Put the baggage on a trolley.

4 Short forms

Read the dialogue again. Find the short forms of these phrases and underline them:

1 There is 2 I cannot 3 I am 4 It is not 5 We do not 6 We are

Now read out the sentences.

5 And now you

What are Liz and Rolf looking forward to doing? Tell your partner one activity you are looking forward to doing on your next holiday: *I'm looking forward to seeing the Pyramids.* Then tell the class what your partner is looking forward to doing: *Peter is looking forward to ...ing ....*

6 3 Introductions

Liz and Rolf arrive at Katy's flat. She introduces them to her boyfriend, Sam. First read the phrases below. Then listen to part one of the dialogue and tick (✓) the phrases you hear.

1 ☐ Let me introduce you to Sam.
2 ☐ Come and meet my parents.
3 ☐ Pleased to meet you.
4 ☐ This is Sam.
5 ☐ Nice to meet you.
6 ☐ How do you do?
7 ☐ Hi. My name's Sam.
8 ☐ Please, call me Liz.

7 4 True or false?

Listen to part two of the dialogue and write if the sentences are true (T) or false (F).

1 Sam is a radiologist. ( )
2 Sam works in a hospital in Bradford. ( )
3 Sam is Scottish. ( )
4 Liz is an interpreter. ( )
5 Rolf works in Stuttgart. ( )
6 Sam has a new MG. ( )
7 There's a transport museum in Edinburgh. ( )

Compare your answers with a partner and correct the sentences which are false. Use *isn't* or *doesn't* in the first part of your answer: *Sam isn't Liz's boyfriend, he's Katy's boyfriend. / He doesn't work in Stuttgart, he works in Edinburgh.*

Remember: *Er ist Arzt. – He is a doctor.*

1

2

3

8 What do they do?

Ask and answer questions about people's jobs: *What does Katy do? She's a student.* And Liz? Rolf? Sam? Now ask about these people.

9 Find someone who ...

Walk round and ask other members of the class questions beginning with *Do you ...?* They will answer with *Yes, I do* or *No, I don't*. When you get a *Yes* answer, write that person's name on the line. You need one name in each space.

1 .... work with computers.
2 .... have a mobile phone.
3 .... work at weekends.
4 .... live in a flat.
5 .... drive a German car.
6 .... drive to work.

Read out one piece of information about two people in your class: *Peter and Nicola both work with computers.*

10 What to say

Ask your partner these questions. Then tell the class two things you found out about your partner.

1 What's your family name? 2 Where are you from? 3 What do you do at weekends? 4 What do you do?

Now look at the Language Focus on page 41 of Pocket Tourist.

UNIT 1
ARRIVAL

SELFSTUDY

In Unit 1 haben Sie gelernt wie man: • Leute begrüßt • sich und Andere vorstellt • Fragen zur eigenen Person stellt und beantwortet und • mit dem *present simple* Gewohnheiten ausdrückt. Üben Sie nun, was Sie gelernt haben:

Eilean Donan Castle, Scotland

1 Scotland

Setzen Sie die richtigen Verbformen ein:

Scotland (1 *be*) .... a very beautiful country. It (2 *have*) .... wonderful lakes, which the Scots (3 *call*) .... lochs, and many islands and mountains. It (4 *not have*) .... high mountains like the Alps – the highest (5 *be*) .... Ben Nevis at 1343 metres – but people (6 *ski*) .... there when it (7 *snow*) .... It (8 *snow*) .... a lot in winter – and it often (9 *rain*) .... in summer! I'm sure you (10 *know*) .... most Scottish people (11 *not wear*) .... kilts every day and they (12 *not play*) .... the bagpipes. But what (13 *eat*) .... a typical Scot ....? Haggis, of course – and he (14 *drink*) .... whisky! (15 *know*) .... you .... what haggis is?

Haggis: ein schottisches Gericht, das aus zerkleinerten Schafsinnereien zubereitet wird (Herz, Lunge, Leber). Sie werden mit Hafermehl und Nierenfett vermischt und in einem Schafsmagen gekocht.

2 5 Listen and repeat

Sprechen Sie die Sätze nach.

1 Wonderful to see you!
2 How are you?
3 I'm fine, thanks. And you?
4 I'm very well, thank you.
5 We're looking forward to meeting him.
6 Let me introduce you to Sam.
7 This is Sam.
8 Pleased to meet you.
9 How do you do?
10 Please, call me Liz.

3 Mix and match

Ordnen Sie die Antworten zu den Fragen.

1 How do you do?	a I'm from Germany.
2 What do you do?	b No, I'm not.
3 How are you?	c I'm an engineer.
4 Where are you from?	d It's Moers.
5 What's your family name?	e How do you do?
6 Are you Scottish?	f I'm fine, thanks.

LANGUAGE AND CULTURE

In many English-speaking countries, most people only shake hands when they are formally introduced, for example, in a business situation – or meeting the girlfriend's parents for the first time! And remember, when someone formally greets you with *"How do you do?"*, you should answer, *"How do you do?"* But in most informal situations you can just smile and say, *"Hello, nice to meet you."* People don't normally shake hands when they greet their friends or say goodbye.

When Katy's mother is introduced to Sam, she says, *"Please, call me Liz."* First names are often used both in social situations and in business.

4 Write the questions

Streichen Sie das jeweils falsche Wort.

1 *Do / Does* he work in Stuttgart?
2 Is he *a / an* engineer?
3 *What / How* is his name?
4 *Do / Does* they live in a flat?
5 *Is / Are* they German?
6 Does he *have / has* a car?
7 Does Katy *drive / drives*?
8 Where *do / does* you live?
9 Are you looking forward to *fly / flying*?

5 Questions with *Wh ...* ?

Stellen Sie Fragen über Rolf, die mit *Wh...* beginnen. Hier sind die dazugehörigen Antworten.

1 Wh..?
His name's Moers.

2 Wh..?
He lives in Stuttgart.

3 Wh..?
He comes from Germany.

4 Wh..?
He's an engineer.

6 Talking about Liz

Lesen Sie, was Liz sagt. Bilden Sie dann Sätze über Liz, indem Sie die markierten Wörter benutzen, z.B. 1 *Liz is English.*

"I am (1) *English* but I live in (2) *Stuttgart*. I'm (3) *married* and I have one (4) *daughter and a son*. I work for the same company as my husband but I don't always work in (5) *Stuttgart*. I'm an interpreter so I travel a lot and I really like my (6) *job*. I speak German, (7) *French* and, of course, English. And I'm looking forward to going to (8) *Italy* next year and learning a bit of Italian."

7 Talking about Katy

Lesen Sie die Informationen auf Seite 8 und beantworten Sie folgende Fragen mit Kurzantworten.

1 Can Katy speak German?

....

2 Is her mother German?

....

3 Does Katy want to be an interpreter?

....

4 Is she a student?

....

5 Are Katy and Sam married?

....

6 Do they share a flat?

....

7 Do Katy's parents live in Scotland?

....

p. 83

Ben Nevis, Scotland

TOURIST TIP

Ask a Scot how high Ben Nevis is and he will probably say: *About 4,400 feet.* Many English-speaking countries don't use the metric system. In Britain the metric system has been introduced but a lot of people still think in the "old" system of yards, feet and inches. Remember: In English, there's a comma after the thousands. Look at page 11 of Pocket Tourist for more information.

UNIT 2
WHAT'S ON

A pub in Edinburgh

1 Starter

Ask and answer questions about local opening and closing times.

A: *What time does your local pub (open)?*
B: *It (opens) at (half past six) in the evening.*

Here are some ideas: bank / supermarket / school / bakery / library / post office

> **Remember:** *<u>in</u> the morning, <u>in</u> the afternoon, <u>in</u> the evening, <u>at</u> night.*

2 6 Let's do that!

Sam: Oh yes, there are lots of things to see in Edinburgh.

Liz: I know there's a lovely cathedral here.

Sam: Actually, there are two cathedrals – Saint Giles' and Saint Mary's. And there's the famous castle, of course. And we could go on a day trip to a loch. I'm free on Tuesday – we could go then.

Rolf: Yes, let's do that – let's go to Loch Ness! Is there *really* a monster in that lake?

Sam: Ah ... there are lots of interesting theories about that! There are some photos of the Loch Ness Monster but I don't think they're authentic. There aren't any very *clear* photos of Nessie.

Liz: No, I'm sure there isn't really a Loch Ness monster – but we could go and look!

Rolf: And what about music? Are there any good concerts at the weekend?

Sam: Oh yes! Edinburgh is *the* place to be in summer! The Edinburgh Festival is on in August, so there are lots of things to do. Why don't we phone the Tourist Hotline? We can find out more information from them.

Liz: Good idea!

3 Read and find out

If you want to correct someone, it's polite to start with *Actually* ... . Now read the dialogue again and politely correct the sentences below.

A: *There aren't any good concerts at the weekend.*
B: *Actually, there are some good concerts at the weekend.*

1 There's one cathedral in Edinburgh.
2 Sam is free on Thursday.
3 The Edinburgh Festival is in October.
4 There aren't any photos of Nessie.
5 Sam thinks they're authentic.
6 There are some very clear photos of Nessie.

> **Remember:** use *some* in positive sentences and *any* for questions and negative sentences.

4 Dates

Complete the names of these months and check them with a partner: M _ _, J _ _ _ _ _ _, N _ _ _ _ _ _ _, A _ _ _ _, M _ _ _ _, S _ _ _ _ _ _ _ _, F _ _ _ _ _ _ _, J _ _ _, J _ _ _, A _ _ _ _ _, D _ _ _ _ _ _ _, O _ _ _ _ _ _.

5 Special days

St Andrew's Day, November 30th (Scotland)

(St Andrew's) Day is the (Scottish) national day. It's on (November the thirtieth).

With a partner, take turns to make similar sentences:

1 St David's Day, March 1st (Wales)
2 St George's Day, April 23rd (England)
3 St Patrick's Day, March 17th (Ireland)
4 Canada Day, July 1st (Canada)
5 Independence Day, July 4th (America)
6 Australia Day, January 26th (Australia)
7 Freedom Day, April 27th (South Africa)

And in your country?

6 Places to visit

With a partner, find the ten places to visit in this grid.

Q	C	D	O	L	W	Y	T
T	H	I	C	A	F	E	H
M	U	S	E	U	M	X	E
P	R	C	I	N	E	M	A
U	C	O	P	E	R	A	T
B	H	C	J	L	F	Z	R
G	A	L	L	E	R	Y	E
U	S	C	A	S	T	L	E

7 Suggestions

Work with a partner. In turns, suggest visiting some of the above places. React to your partner's suggestions with: ☺ *That's a good idea!* or ☹ *Actually, I don't really fancy that, but we could go to the ... .*

Let's go to the ... **Why don't we go to the ...** **We could go to the ...**	**...**	**on**	**Monday.** **Tuesday.** **Wednesday.** **Thursday.** **Friday.** **Saturday.** **Sunday.**
		at	**the weekend.**

Now tell the class where you and your partner want to go and when: *We want to go to... on/at ... .*

8 Memory game

Your teacher will write these phrases on the board:

- *There is(n't) a/an ... .*
- *There aren't any ... .*
- *There are some ... .*
- *There are lots of... .*

Call out as many sentences as you can about your town, like this: *There are lots of theatres in this town.*

Now your teacher will divide the class into two teams, A and B. Both teams, please turn to page 75 and look at the map of Glenfellet.

9 7 Tourist Hotline

Liz and Rolf want to find out what there is to see and do in Edinburgh, so they phone the Edinburgh Royal Mile Tourist Hotline. Listen to the dialogue and make notes about the following information.

1 Which number do you press for 'What's on' information?
2 What time does the castle open and close in summer?
3 What day does the Whisky Heritage Centre close?
4 When is the cathedral concert?
5 Where and when do the ghost tours begin?

Tell the class what you've found out.

Now look at the Language Focus on page 42 of Pocket Tourist.

SELFSTUDY

In Unit 2 haben Sie gelernt wie man: • Zeit und Datum ausdrückt • sagt, wann etwas passiert ist • Vorschläge macht und darauf reagiert und • was man in Städten unternehmen kann.
Üben Sie nun, was Sie gelernt haben.

1 Royal Yacht Britannia

Ergänzen Sie die Wörter:
a, an, some (2x), any, lots of.

Royal Yacht Britannia

The Royal Yacht Britannia is now one of Scotland's biggest tourist attractions. It is visited by (1) .... tourists – over 300,000 every year! They come to see how the Royal Family lived during (2) .... of their state visits to Commonwealth countries. There is (3) .... elegant state dining room where the Queen entertained (4) .... of the world's leaders, including Margaret Thatcher, Nelson Mandela and Bill Clinton. Today there aren't (5) .... royal banquets on the yacht but it is possible for companies to organise (6) .... private dinner on board.

2 8 Listen and repeat

Sprechen Sie die Sätze nach.

1 There are lots of things to see.
2 There's a famous castle.
3 We could go on a day trip.
4 Let's do that.
5 Actually, I don't really fancy that.
6 Why don't we phone?
7 Good idea!
8 Are there any good concerts at the weekend?
9 There are some photos of Nessie.
10 There aren't any clear photos.

3 What's wrong?

Streichen Sie die falschen Wörter.

1 11.40 is twenty to twelve *in the* / *at* night.
2 7.15 is quarter *to* / *past* seven.
3 11.30 is half past *twelve* / *eleven*.
4 My train leaves *on* / *at* 2 o'clock.

LANGUAGE AND CULTURE

The 24-hour clock is not used as often in Britain as on the Continent. If you need to make the difference clear between 8.00 and 20.00 you can of course say eight o'clock *in the morning* or eight o'clock *in the evening*. But you can also use *a.m.* (ante meridiem) for 0.00 - 12.00, so 8.00 is 8 a.m.; and you can use *p.m.* (post meridiem) for 12.00 - 24.00, so 20.00 is 8 p.m. 12.00 is midday and 24.00 is midnight:
My plane leaves at midday / midnight.

4 What time do they arrive?

Schreiben Sie die Uhrzeiten in Worten.
14.20: twenty past two in the afternoon.

1 9.30 : ....

....

2 15.15 : ....

....

3 20.35 : ....

....

4 23.05 : ....

....

5 12.00 : ....

....

5 A rainy afternoon

Vervollständigen Sie die Sätze, indem Sie die angegebenen Wörter verwenden.

any / are / an / is / there / a / is / an / some / a / are

A: Let's find somewhere warm and dry – (1) .... there (2) .... museum in this town?

B: Actually, there (3) .... two museums and there is (4) .... art gallery, too. We could go to the gallery this afternoon.

A: Actually, I don't really fancy that. But (5) .... there (6) .... cinema near here?

B: No, (7) .... isn't a cinema in this part of town but there are (8) .... good cinemas in the town centre. Why don't we go to see a film this evening?

A: Good idea. And (9) .... there (10) .... really good restauraunts?

B: Yes, there's (11) .... excellent Indian restaurant near the station. Let's go there for lunch now.

6 Suggestions

Lesen Sie den Dialog in Übung 5 nochmals und notieren Sie drei Möglichkeiten, jemandem etwas vorzuschlagen.

1 ....

2 ....

3 ....

7 9 Say when

Hören Sie die Gespräche im *Tourist Information Office* an und vervollständigen Sie die Sätze.

1 Edinburgh Castle closes a little earlier ....

2 The Hard Rock Café closes ....

3 The Ski Centre is open .... and ....

4 The Golf Club at Braid Hills is also open to visitors ....

5 The National Gallery of Scotland opens at midday ....

National Gallery, Edinburgh

p. 83

TOURIST TIP

Is the country you want to travel to in the same time zone as here? If not, make a note of the time difference on page 42 of Pocket Tourist. Even in European countries, times can be different. What time is it now? In Britain it's one hour earlier!

Table Mountain, Cape Town

UNIT 3

A GUIDED TOUR

Thailand

1 Starter

Tell the class where you were on your last holiday, when you were there and say one thing about it.

I was in (Thailand) (3 months) ago and it was (fantastic).

2 A visit to the distillery

On Saturday afternoon Liz and Rolf visited the Glenfellet Whisky Distillery. They brought this leaflet back with them and showed it to Katy and Sam.

Glenfellet – established in 1785 – is one of Scotland's oldest whisky distilleries.

Visitors Centre

- Open 7 days
- Guided tours (in English only)
- Free tasting of the Glenfellet Single Highland Malt Scotch – one of Scotland's finest whiskies
- Audio-visual presentation about whisky-making (in English, German, French and Japanese)
- 2 restaurants beside the River Glenfellet
- Gift shop

Opening times – February to December
Monday to Saturday 9.30 a.m. – 6.00 p.m.
(last tour 4.30 p.m.)

3 Ask the question

Complete the questions using *Was* or *Were*. Then ask the questions to another member of the class. He / She will answer with *Yes, there was / were* or *No, there wasn't / weren't.*

1 .... there any guided tours in German?

2 .... there a free whisky tasting?

3 .... there an audio-visual presentation in German?

4 .... there any cafés or restaurants?

5 .... there a gift shop?

6 .... there a tour after five o'clock?

4 Describing things

Tick (✓) which adjectives you can use with each of the nouns. Then compare your answers with a partner.

	awful	delicious	friendly	comfortable	marvellous	expensive
food						
people						
hotel						
weather						
shops						
scenery						
public transport						

5 Opposites

Find the opposite adjectives and join them with a line.

1 hot	good
2 expensive	ugly
3 bad	uncomfortable
4 new	poor
5 pretty	old
6 rich	cheap
7 comfortable	cold

Now choose four of these adjectives. Write them down on a piece of paper and ask a partner to write the comparative and superlative forms of each adjective, like this:

old, older, oldest / easy, easier, easiest / difficult, more difficult, most difficult

6 What was it like?

Ask someone in your class: *What was your best / worst holiday?* Then ask questions about that holiday. You can use words from activities 4 and 5.

A: *What was the food like?* B: *It was delicious!*

7 10 Ordering drinks

Liz and Rolf meet Katy and Sam in a pub and they order some drinks. First read the phrases below. Then listen to the dialogue and number the phrases in the order in which you hear them.

Remember:
I'd like to taste it. / I'd like a coke. *'d* = would

- ☐ Could you get me a glass of coke, please?
- ☐ What would you like?
- ☐ Just a half for me, please.
- ☐ I'd like a gin and tonic, please.
- ☐ I'd like to try a Guinness.
- ☐ Could I have a packet of crisps, please?

Remember: *ein Glas Cola - a glass of coke*

8 10 Who ordered what?

Listen to the dialogue again and write the name *Liz, Rolf, Katy* or *Sam* next to any items asked for.

glass of coke ______
large whisky ______
half a pint of Guinness ______
gin and tonic ______
packet of peanuts ______
ice and lemon ______
packet of crisps ______
bottle of low alcohol lager ______

9 What would you say?

What do you think Sam said when he went to get the drinks at the bar? Now work with a partner. How would you ask for these things in a pub?

10 11 Chatting in the pub

Listen to Liz and Rolf telling Katy and Sam about their visit to the whisky distillery. Write the missing words in the sentences below.

1 We both had a really .... time.

2 It's one of the .... distilleries in Scotland.

3 Their Internet page is very ....

4 The food was ....

5 One restaurant was a bit ....

6 The self-service restaurant was ....

7 And the menu looked ....

Replace each adjective you wrote with a different one. Then read one sentence to the class.

Now look at the Language Focus on page 43 of Pocket Tourist.

UNIT 3
A GUIDED TOUR

Golf is played everywhere in Scotland

SELFSTUDY

In Unit 3 haben Sie gelernt wie man: • mit *was* und *were* über Vergangenes spricht • Gefallen oder Missfallen ausdrückt • nach etwas fragt und • Vergleiche anstellt. Üben Sie nun, was Sie gelernt haben.

1 Golfing in Scotland

St Andrews Golf Club

Setzen Sie die richtige Form des jeweiligen Adjektivs ein, z.B. *famous, more famous, most famous.*

Scotland is (1 *famous*) ...famous... for its golf courses. The golf course at St Andrews is the (2 *famous*) .... but the (3 *old*) .... golf course in the world is in Musselburgh, a (4 *small*) .... town near Edinburgh. Originally it only had 7 holes but, in 1870, it was made (5 *big*) .... and it now has 9 holes. Some of the world's (6 *good*) .... golfers have played there – Willie Park Junior, Deacon Brown and Bob Furguson. But perhaps the (7 *surprising*) .... player was Mary, Queen of Scots, who played there in 1567.

LANGUAGE AND CULTURE

In British pubs you normally order and pay for drinks and snacks at the bar. If you are with a group, you *'buy a round'* – that means to order and pay for a drink for everyone in your group. This makes things both simpler and quicker at the bar. Children are not allowed to go in most pubs. And the landlord (the owner of the pub) will not serve alcohol to people under eighteen.

2 12 Listen and repeat

Sprechen Sie die Sätze nach.

1 I was in Spain three months ago.
2 What were the people like?
3 They were really friendly.
4 The weather was better than here.
5 What would you like to drink?
6 I'd like a gin and tonic, please.
7 Could you get me a glass of coke, please?
8 A pint of lager for me.
9 Could I have a packet of crisps, please?
10 I'd like to try a Guinness.

3 Mix and match

Kombinieren Sie die richtigen Satzhälften.

1 I'd like a	☐	a	have a drink, please?
2 Could I	☐	b	gin and tonic, please.
3 I'd like	☐	c	of lager for me.
4 Could	☐	d	to try that.
5 A pint	☐	e	you get me a glass of coke, please?

4 A letter home

Vervollständigen Sie den Brief von Liz. Benutzen Sie *was, wasn't, were* und *weren't.*

And, do you know, the whisky-tasting (1) .... free! There (2) .... lots of different sorts and Rolf says they (3) .... all marvellous! You know I don't like whisky, so I (4) .... interested in the tasting - I (5) .... in the gift shop, of course. And where (6) .... Katy and Sam? They (7) .... with us - they (8) .... in town, shopping for their trip to Australia. But we (9) .... all together in the pub later. It (10) .... a really wonderful day!

Love to all,

Liz

5 What's the word?

Welche Adjektive verbergen sich hinter diesen Buchstaben? Schreiben Sie sie in die erste Spalte der Tabelle.

1 gib 2 indefrly 3 itnesrngeti 4 ogod 5 abd

	adjective	comparative	superlative
	nice	nicer	nicest
1			
2			
3			
4			
5			

Ergänzen Sie nun die Steigerungsformen der Adjektive in der Tabelle.

6 Questions

Bilden Sie Fragesätze.

1 in/Where/you/were/summer

.... ?

2 very/hotel/your/expensive/Was

.... ?

3 the/Was/here/weather/than/worse

.... ?

4 people/like/were/What/the

.... ?

5 would/to/drink/you/What/like

.... ?

6 Could/me/bring/a/and/tonic/please/gin/you

.... ?

7 I/a/have/beer/Could/pint/please/of

.... ?

8 you/a/like/Would/lager

.... ?

p. 83

TOURIST TIP

In many English-speaking countries, pubs and bars don't use litres. They sell drinks in *pints* and *half pints*. But the British pint (0.568 litres) is not the same as the American pint (0.473 liters). Look at page 29 of Pocket Tourist for more information.

UNIT 4
LOCH NESS

Loch Ness

1 Starter

Remember: 1999: Nineteen ~~hundred~~ ninety-nine.

Make up a long sentence about a holiday, like this:

A: *I went to (Scotland) in (1999).*
B: *I went to Scotland in 1999 and I travelled by (car).*
C: *I went to Scotland in 1999; I travelled by car and I stayed for (two weeks).*
D: *I went to Scotland in 1999; I travelled by car; I stayed for two weeks and I saw (the Loch Ness monster)!*

Use these verbs: *went, travelled, stayed, saw*. Then the next person begins a new sentence.

2 Liz's diary

Liz writes in her diary every day. Read what she wrote on Tuesday evening.

Tuesday:

We went to Loch Ness today and we really enjoyed ourselves – but no, we didn't see Nessie! We took the train to Inverness and then Sam's friend Andrew met us at the station. He took us by car to Drumnadrochit, a village beside the loch, where we spent an hour in the Visitors Centre and then went for a boat trip on the ~~lake~~ loch. The scenery was marvellous – lots of beautiful mountains and castles – and we had lunch in a lovely country pub. Rolf drank whisky, of course, and we ate a local speciality – fresh fish from the loch. We sent some postcards and we bought a painting of Loch Ness as a souvenir. Katy took lots of photos – I'm looking forward to seeing them! There were some photos of Nessie (authentic or not!) on the walls and we met some of the local people. They told us stories about the Loch Ness monster and other famous Scottish tales – including the history of Gretna Green. And why did Sam want to know so much about Gretna Green, I ask myself?

3 Read and remember

Read Liz's diary. Now cover up the text and correct these sentences, like this:

They went to Loch Lomond. – They didn't go to Loch Lomond, they went to Loch Ness.

1 They went to Inverness by car.
2 They travelled to Drumnadrochit by bus.
3 They saw beautiful rivers and waterfalls.
4 They had lunch in a hotel.
5 Rolf drank wine.
6 They ate haggis.
7 They bought a photo of Loch Ness.

4 My best holiday

Complete these sentences about your best holiday, like this: *I went to* ..India... *in* ..2001...

I went to (1) .... in (2) .... and I stayed there for (3) .... I travelled by (4) .... and I saw (5) .... I ate lots of (6) .... and drank (7) .... The weather was (8) .... and the people were (9) .... I bought (10) .... I really enjoyed myself.

5 Find out

Work with a partner and write the questions you would ask to find out the information in Activity 4.

Remember: To ask questions about the past, use *did*, *was* or *were*.

Canada

Thailand

Ask a different partner these questions to find out information about his / her best holiday:

A: *Where did you go?* B: *I went to Egypt.*
A: *When did you go there?* B: ...
A: *How long ... ?*

6 Do-it-yourself!

Match the two parts of the phrases.

1 We really enjoyed	☐	a himself.
2 Goodbye, Katy. Look after	☐	b herself.
3 He enjoyed	☐	c ourselves.
4 They didn't hurt	☐	d yourselves.
5 Bye, Katy. Bye, Sam. Look after	☐	e themselves.
6 She hurt	☐	f myself.
7 Thank you. I really enjoyed	☐	g yourself.

Egypt

7 Talk about it

Work in small groups and say what kind of holidays you prefer.
Do it like this:

I (don't) like .... holidays because: you have to ... / don't have to ... / you can ... / you can't ... .

Here are some kinds of holiday to talk about: *camping, hotel, package, family, cycling, bed and breakfast, walking, sight-seeing, bus-tour, language-learning, skiing, fly and drive, self-catering.*

8 13 Buying a ticket

On Monday evening Katy went to the station and bought the train tickets for Inverness.

First read these sentences. Now listen to the conversation and underline the phrases you hear:

I'd like four single/return tickets to Inverness, please.

1. We want to travel on *Tuesday / Thursday*.
2. Are there any *special offers / cheap-rate tickets*?
3. There are cheaper tickets if you travel *at the weekend / after nine o'clock*.
4. That's the *8.14 / 8.40* from Edinburgh Waverley.
5. You *have to / don't have to* change.
6. Could I *reserve / book* four seats, please?
7. Four seats in *smoking / non-smoking* accommodation.
8. Is there a train which *gets back to / arrives in* Edinburgh in the evening?
9. How long *is the journey / does the journey take*?
10. Just *over / under* three hours.

9 And now you

The class will be split into pairs, student A and student B.
A students, please look at page 76. B students, please look at page 78.

Now look at the Language Focus on page 44 of Pocket Tourist.

UNIT 4
LOCH NESS

Getting married in Gretna Green

SELFSTUDY

In Unit 4, haben Sie gelernt wie man: • mit dem *past simple* über einen vergangenen Urlaub spricht • Reflexivpronomen anwendet • eine Zugfahrkarte reserviert und • mit *have to* über Pflichten spricht. Üben Sie nun, was Sie gelernt haben.

1 Gretna Green

Ergänzen Sie die passenden Verbformen im *past simple*.

Why (1 *ask*) .... Sam .... for information about Gretna Green? Maybe he is interested in weddings? Gretna Green, a Scottish village just over the border from England, is famous for weddings. This (2 *start*) .... over 350 years ago. In England young people couldn't get married if their father (3 *not want*) .... them to – so young people often (4 *run*) .... away to Scotland, where it (5 *be*) .... easier to get married. In the 1650s, a rich young German man from Moravia[1] (6 *go*) .... to visit friends in the North of England. There he (7 *meet*) .... a young woman and they (8 *fall*) .... in love. He (9 *tell*) .... the girl's father he (10 *want*) .... to marry her but her father (11 *say*) .... no. So the young couple (12 *ride*) .... to Gretna Green and (13 *get*) .... married. The woman's father (14 follow) .... them and (15 *try*) .... to stop the wedding. But he (16 *not find*) .... them in time. The married couple then (17 *leave*) .... England and (18 *go*) .... to live in Germany.

2 14 Listen and repeat

Sprechen Sie die Sätze nach.

1 I went to India in 1999.
2 I really enjoyed myself.
3 We travelled by train.
4 We didn't go by bus.
5 We didn't have to change.
6 How long did you stay there?
7 I'd like a return ticket to Inverness, please.
8 Do we have to change?
9 How long does the journey take?
10 Bye. Look after yourselves.

[1] Moravia: now part of Czech Republic

3 Self help

Vervollständigen Sie die Sätze mit einem Fürwort, das auf *-self* oder *-selves* endet.

1 In a self-service restaurant, the customers have to serve ....
2 We enjoyed .... at the party.
3 He's self-employed – he works for ....
4 Do you ever talk to .... ?
5 She hurt .... in the swimming pool.

LANGUAGE AND CULTURE

When you travel to English-speaking countries, don't be surprised if there are some words which you don't understand at first. For example, you now know that the Scottish word for *lake* is *"loch"*. Some countries have adopted American English and some speak British English. When you book a ticket, in B.E. you would ask for a *single* or a *return* ticket; in A.E. you would ask for a *one-way* or a *round trip* ticket. Do you know who would put their *baggage* into a *cab* and who would put their *luggage* into a *taxi*?

p. 84

4 You have to do it

Vervollständigen Sie die Sätze. Benutzen Sie eine positive oder negative Form von *have to* und eines der angegeben Verben.

drive / pay / book / change / explain

1 It's a direct train so they don't have to change

2 When you don't understand something, your teacher ....

....

3 When Rolf has drunk whisky, Liz ....

....

4 There are always lots of seats so you ....

....

5 Children under twelve are free – they ....

....

TOURIST TIP

Travelling by public transport is usually much cheaper if you book in advance or use a travel pass. Try to find out as much information as possible before you leave home.
You could use the Internet, perhaps. In many countries you can now book and pay online for tickets.

5 Goodbye

Katy und Sam fahren nach Australien. Liz und Rolf verabschieden sich von Ihnen am Flughafen. Versuchen Sie die fehlenden Wörter zu ergänzen.

1 K: Sam has the _ i _ _ e _ _ and the passports.

2 L: Look a _ _ e_ yourselves.

3 S: I'm looking _ o _ _ a _ _ to it.

4 K: I don't _ a _ e to work.

5 L: Have a _ i _ e time, Katy.

6 R: E _ _ o _ yourself, Sam.

7 L: Send us a _ o _ _ _ a _ _.

8 K: See you in _ o u _ weeks.

6 Mix and match

Finden Sie die richtigen Antworten auf die Fragen.

1 Are there any cheap-rate tickets?	a ☐	Er, no – a single, please.
2 What time does it get to Edinburgh?	b ☐	It departs Glasgow Central, 18.45.
3 Would you like a return?	c ☐	Yes, of course. Non-smoking?
4 How long does the journey take?	d ☐	No, you don't – it's a direct train.
5 Do I have to change?	e ☐	It arrives at 13.20.
6 What time does it leave?	f ☐	Sorry, it's full-price at the weekend.
7 Could I reserve two seats, please?	g ☐	About two hours.

p. 84

AMERICAN HIGHLIGHTS
AMERICAN HIGHLIGHTS

Have you ever been to America? If you have, tell the class about some of your experiences. Which images come into your mind when you hear the word *America*?

The Capitol, Washington D.C.

THE STARS AND STRIPES

America is a vast country with huge social, geographical and cultural variety, united under one president and under one flag: the *Stars and Stripes*. The first flag was made in 1717 when there were thirteen states. The thirteen stripes represent those original states and the 50 stars represent the number of states in America today.

Native American Indian

NATIVE AMERICANS

At the beginning of the 1600s, Indians welcomed and helped the early settlers in America. But the Europeans took land from the "Redskins" and massacred thousands of them. Until very recently – 1924 – Indians were not allowed to become American citizens. Today Indian culture fascinates more and more people and and there are Native American festivals all through the year, where visitors can buy traditional art work and watch Indian ceremonies.

HOLLYWOOD

Hollywood is the centre of the world's film industry. One (free!) tourist attraction in Hollywood is *Grauman's Chinese Theater*. Since this movie theatre opened in 1927, nearly 200 stars have written their names in wet concrete in front of the exotic, pagoda-shaped[1] cinema. And every year two million visitors go to see the autographs, handprints and footprints of stars like Frank Sinatra, Marilyn Monroe, Liz Taylor, Steven Spielberg, John Wayne and Cary Grant.

1 pagoda-shaped: Pavillon-artig

CASINOS AND WEDDINGS

Which city comes to mind? Las Vegas, of course. In 1931, to make money for the state, gambling was legalised in Nevada and Las Vegas became the casino capital of the world. A huge entertainment industry has developed with exotic hotels and enormous gambling halls. Las Vegas also has very liberal marriage (and divorce!) laws. Over 100,000 couples get married here every year. The couple can choose a traditional wedding or a theme wedding – an Elvis look-alike wedding, a marriage in Camelot, a rodeo, a Harley Davidson motorbike wedding or a casino ceremony.

THE STREETS OF SAN FRANCISCO

We've probably all seen films with car chases through the hilly streets of San Francisco. The crowded cable cars, the elegant houses and the Golden Gate Bridge are familiar to us even if we have never been to San Francisco. But the main attraction for 87% of the tourists in San Francisco is Fisherman's Wharf, where the restaurants serve freshly caught fish and a special kind of local bread. Tourists can also enjoy boat trips around the harbour – or sail the 2 kilometres to the old prison island of Alcatraz, where Al Capone was in prison.

Arches National Park, USA

NATIONAL PARKS

The scenery in America is breathtaking. The Grand Canyon is one of the seven natural wonders of the world. The Yosemite National Park in California with its giant sequoia trees is 3080 square kilometres - bigger than the Saarland. Death Valley National Park has an average temperature of 47°C in July – and yet 900 different species of plants grow there. The rock formations in Antelope Canyon make it a paradise for photographers. The colourful rocks and exotic wildlife in Bryce Canyon attract 1.5 million visitors a year. If you want to see cliffs, caves and canyons, the National Parks are the place to be.

THE STATUE OF LIBERTY

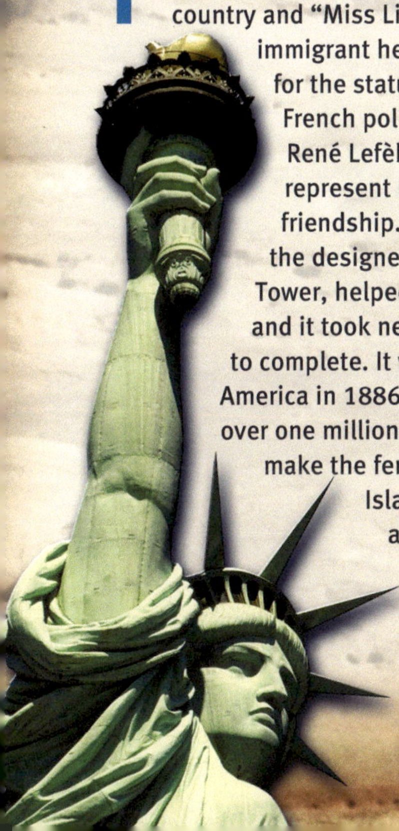

This statue was one of the first sights many immigrants had of their new country and "Miss Liberty" was an immigrant herself. The idea for the statue came from a French politician, Edouard-René Lefèbvre and it was to represent Franco-American friendship. Gustave Eiffel, the designer of the Eiffel Tower, helped to design it and it took nearly 20 years to complete. It was given to America in 1886 and today over one million visitors a year make the ferry trip to Liberty Island and queue at the feet of "Miss Liberty".

PUZZLE CORNER

Can you name the four presidents in the Mount Rushmore National Memorial? Here are their initials to help you:

G _ _ _ _ _ W _ _ _ _ _ _ _ _ _

T _ _ _ _ _ J _ _ _ _ _ _ _ _

T _ _ _ _ _ _ _ R _ _ _ _ _ _ _ _

A _ _ _ _ _ _ L _ _ _ _ _

p. 84

AMERICAN HIGHLIGHTS
SPOTLIGHT ON NEW YORK

Trump Hotel, New York

THE BIG APPLE

The city of New York is also known as the *Big Apple*. This name was adopted in 1971 as part of a campaign to attract more tourists to New York. But no-one is sure where the phrase *Big Apple* comes from! One theory is that the *Big Apple* was named after a kind of square dance in the 1930s.

Tourist Tip: The *Big Apple Greeter* is a free public service organised by the city of New York. Tourists can book the service of a New Yorker who will show them round the city for three or four hours and give them insider tips on the many attractions of the city – a city which offers nearly everything to its residents and tourists.

SHOPPING

New York is a mecca for shopoholics! It's the home of the very first department store – the Marble Dry-Goods Palace, which was opened in 1846. Today, Macy's, with 100,000 square metres of shopping space and over 400,000 articles, is the biggest department store in the world. In New York you can find other world-famous department stores like Bloomingdale's, Saks and Tiffany's, hundreds of exclusive boutiques, and masses of designer clothes. You can buy almost anything in New York – for example, at Hammacher Schlemmer, you can even buy a real submarine!

Tourist Tip: Don't miss Manhattan's flea markets, where you can buy both second-hand and new items at cheap prices.

ENTERTAINMENT

On Broadway, musicals like *Cats*, *Miss Saigon* and *42nd Street* have broken all records and over 11,000,000 tickets a year are sold for Broadway shows. If classical music is more your style, visit the Metropolitan Opera in New York – it's the largest opera house in the world with 4,065 seats.

Tourist Tip: Buy the magazine *Time out* to find out what's on – or log on to one of the 30,000,000 websites about New York.

HOTELS

There are lots of exclusive – and expensive! – hotels in NY: the Plaza Hotel, where Mark Twain, Eleanor Roosevelt and architect Frank Lloyd Wright liked to stay; and the Waldorf Astoria, the hotel for visiting diplomats, princes, prime ministers and presidents. In the 1890s the Waldorf gave its name to the *Waldorf Salad*, a salad of apples, celery and nuts. The Pennsylvania Hotel was made internationally famous by the Glenn Miller's Orchestra hit *Pennsylvania 65 000* – and that is still the telephone number of the hotel today.

Tourist Tip: When you book a hotel, ask if they have "special rates" or "package deals" – these are cheaper than the normal prices.

Metropolitan Museum, New York

CULTURE

The American Museum of Natural History is the biggest museum in the world (11,148 square metres) and houses the skeleton of the biggest dinosaur in the world. There are nearly 400 museums in New York, and several of them – including the Guggenheim Museum in the unusual building designed by Frank Lloyd Wright, and the Metropolitan Museum of Art with the largest collection of art in America – can be found along Museum Mile on Fifth Avenue. So whether you want to see comic books or pianos, golf balls or menus, New York has a museum for you.

Tourist Tip: Remember that most museums and galleries are closed on Mondays.

PARKS

New York has 1,543 public parks and playgrounds and the largest is Central Park – with 3.4 million square metres. Fifteen million people visit this park every year – to play hockey, listen to concerts (there are free open-air concerts in summer), go jogging, visit the wildlife centre, have picnics, look at flowers – and even get married! One very attractive place is the Shakespeare Garden. Here you can see all the trees and flowers which Shakespeare mentioned in his works.

Tourist Tip: The crime rate in New York is not as high as it was but there are certain areas of the park – and of the city – which you shouldn't go to at night. Check with the local residents or ask at your hotel if you plan to go for a walk in the evening.

Central Park

LANGUAGE CORNER

New York was originally called Nieuw Amsterdam because the first European settlers there were Dutch. There were many different European settlers in America and this influenced American English so it developed differently from British English. There were a lot of German immigrants – and even today an American might say "Gesundheit!", not "Bless you!" if you sneeze!

Can you match the American words and phrases with the British words and phrases?

1 freeway	☐ a petrol
2 cab	☐ b holiday
3 fall	☐ c lift
4 gas	☐ d motorway
5 baggage	☐ e bill
6 stand in line	☐ f ground floor
7 vacation	☐ g taxi
8 bathroom	☐ h queue
9 elevator	☐ i toilet
10 first floor	☐ j handbag
11 check	☐ k autumn
12 purse	☐ l luggage

p. 84

The Adventures of Ivor Problem and Annie Mergency

THE BREAKDOWN

Ivor Problem und Annie Mergency sind in Großbritannien im Urlaub. Auf der Autobahn haben sie plötzlich Probleme ...

Wenn Sie die Geschichte lesen, aufschreiben oder nachspielen, können Sie die markierten Ausdrücke durch jeweils einen anderen Ausdruck in der gleichen Farbe ersetzen. Weitere nützliche Wörter und Redewendungen zum Thema Verkehr finden Sie in Pocket Tourist auf den Seiten 14-15.

brakes, steering	a BMW, an MG	wrong, the matter
Let's, Why don't we	H 359 GJK, F 440 SPG	fix, mend

Thanks a lot, Thank you	get petrol, fill the tank	terribly, awfully
It's all right, You're welcome	Be careful!, Watch out!	It doesen't matter, Never mind

WELCOME TO AUSTRALIA

Katy and Sam arrive in Sydney one day before the medical conference which Sam has to attend. After the conference they enjoy some of Australia's attractions: they have a typical Australian meal with some of Sam's colleagues and they climb the famous Sydney Harbour Bridge. They hire a car for the weekend to drive to Parramatta, where they go hot-air ballooning and get a bird's-eye view of the wonderful Blue Mountains.

Sydney Opera House

An Aborigine with traditional crafts

Bondi Beach, Sydney

UNIT 5
DOWN UNDER

Sydney

1 Starter

The international dialling code from Europe to Australia is: 0061 (zero zero six one). Do you know the code for any other countries?

2 15 Our case is missing!

Katy and Sam arrive in Sydney for the medical conference where Sam has to give a presentation. At the airport they wait for their suitcases in baggage reclaim – but one case is missing – the case with Sam's lecture notes in it!

Sam: Is *that* case ours?

Katy: No, look, it's theirs. Ours has a leather strap. It isn't here, Sam. And the carousel's empty now.

Sam: Oh hell! All my lecture notes are in that case.

Katy: And all our clothes are in it, too.

Sam: *And* my brother's camera ...

Katy: Pardon?

Sam: Yes, Simon's camera's in that case. I borrowed his digital camera for the trip.

Katy: Oh, no. Come on, Sam, let's go and report it.

Sam: Excuse me!

Airline representative: G'day. Can I help you?

Sam: I hope so! One of our cases is missing. This case arrived all right - and my girlfriend has hers, but our big suitcase is missing. It's a grey Samsonite®. And it has some very important papers in it.

AR: Which flight were you on?

Sam: Our last flight was with Qantas Airlines from Bangkok to Sydney. But we left Edinburgh on the 8 p.m. BA flight to London on Saturday and then flew to Bangkok. Look, these papers are really important. I have to give a lecture tomorrow and I need my lecture notes!

AR: Look, I'm terribly sorry sir, but don't worry – the case is probably on the next flight.

Sam: Probably!!

Katy: So what do we do now?

AR: Well, you have to fill in this form, giving details of your flight numbers and what was in the case and the address of your hotel ...

Sam: Give me the form, Katy. You telephone home. The disk with my lecture notes on it is on my computer desk – your father can send the document by e-mail. Do you know the code for Britain?

Katy: But, Sam, it's one o'clock in the morning there!

3 Questions and answers

Put one of these question words at the beginning of each question. You can use each word only once:
Which / Where / How / Who / What / When / Whose

1 .... colour is their lost case?

2 .... airlines did Katy and Sam travel with?

3 .... many flights were they on?

4 .... did they leave Edinburgh?

5 .... are Sam's lecture notes?

6 .... digital camera is it?

7 .... is Simon?

Now ask the questions to other members of the class.

> **Remember:** Simon is Sam's brother.
> NOT: Simon ~~is the brother of Sam.~~

4 Suitcase Bingo

Tell the class one thing you pack in your suitcase when you go on holiday.

> **Remember:** *trousers / shorts / jeans / sunglasses* are plural nouns: NOT: ~~*a*~~ *jeans*, but *a pair of jeans, two pairs of shorts etc.*

Now look at page 81 and have a game of suitcase bingo.

5 The family

With a partner, complete this table.

male	female
father	mother
grandfather	
	wife
	aunt
son	
	sister
nephew	
	cousin

If you have a photograph of someone in your family, show it to the class, say who it is and say something more about this person's family: *This is my brother Joe. He's married and he has a son – my nephew, Peter.*

6 16 Sam's family

Listen to Sam talking about his family. Fill in the missing names on his family tree.

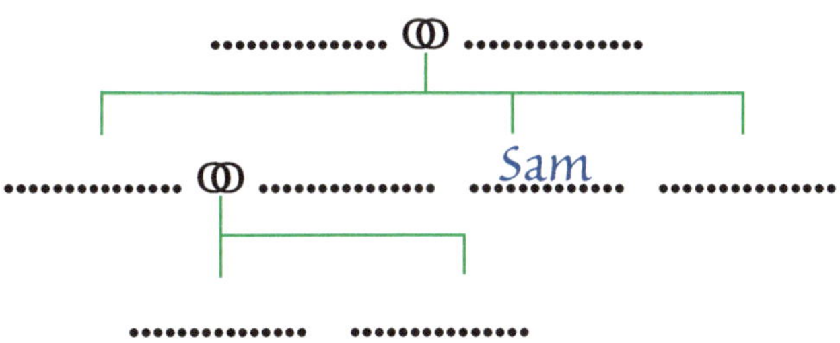

Write down what relation these people are to Sam:

Mary is Sam's mother.

1 Alex ....

2 Sarah ....

3 Simon ....

4 Emma..

5 Steven ....

Check your answers by asking a partner: *Who is Mary*? Your partner will answer: *She is Sam's mother.*

7 Whose is it?

Your teacher will collect one item from each member of the class. Then he/she will hand an item to a student who will try to find the owner.

A: *Excuse me, Peter. Whose is this (mobile phone)? / Whose are these (cigarettes)?*

B: *I think it's / they're Karl's.*

C: *Yes, that's right. It's / They're mine.*

8 17 Phoning home

Sam's notes for the presentation are in the missing suitcase. Katy phones her parents in Edinburgh to ask if they can send a copy by e-mail. Listen to the conversation and answer the questions.

1 Why does Katy say sorry to her mother?
2 What time is it in Sydney when Katy phones her mother?
3 What does Sam want to wear at the conference?
4 What does Katy ask her Mum and Dad to send?
5 Where can Sam and Katy pick up the documents?
6 How can Liz recognise the disk?

9 17 What did they say?

Now listen to the conversation again and underline exactly what Liz and Katy say.

1 Liz answers the phone: *6-8-4-2-3-3-0, hello?/ Hello, 6-8-4-2-3-3-0.*

2 Katy says who is on the phone: *This is Katy. / Katy here.*

3 Katy wants to speak to her father: *Could I speak to Dad? / Can I speak to Dad?*

4 Liz asks her to wait a minute: *Just a minute. / Hold on a moment.*

10 Phone a friend

Work with a partner. Student A, please look at page 76. Student B, please look at page 78.

Now look at the Language Focus on page 45 of Pocket Tourist.

UNIT 5

DOWN UNDER

SELFSTUDY

In Unit 5 haben Sie gelernt wie man: • die Begriffe *Sorry*, *Pardon* und *Excuse me* verwendet • ausdrückt, wem Dinge gehören • über seine Familie spricht und • ein Telefongespräch führt. Üben Sie nun, was Sie gelernt haben.

1 Saying 'G'day'

Es ist nicht immer wichtig, jedes Wort einer Fremdsprache zu verstehen. Häufig genügt es, die wichtigen Informationen herausfiltern zu können. Lesen Sie diese Bedienungsanleitung eines öffentlichen Telefons in Australien.

Payphone

How to make a call

1 Lift the handset and wait for a dial tone
2 Insert coins in coin slot OR insert card (accepts Telstra Phone card only) in direction of arrow. Minimum fee 40c
3 Dial number

Coin payment information

This payphone will not give change

Accepts all Australian coins

Maximum of 8 coins can be used at once (unused coins will be returned)

Payphone identification number

089335612

This payphone does not accept incoming calls

Sind folgende Sätze wahr (T for true) oder falsch (F for false)?

1 When you hear the dial tone you must first dial the number you want. ( )
2 You can use only one type of phone card in the payphone. ( )
3 You must not insert more than 40c. ( )
4 It is better not to use coins with a high value. ( )
5 If you insert four coins but only use three, you will get one of them back. ( )
6 If you have no more coins, you can ask the person you are phoning to ring you back on the number 089335612. ( )

2 18 Listen and repeat

Sprechen Sie die Sätze nach.

1 What's your phone number?
2 What's the dialling code for Australia, please?
3 Could I speak to Katy, please?
4 Whose is it?
5 It isn't mine.
6 Is it yours?
7 That's my sister's case.
8 I'm sorry, I don't know.
9 Pardon? Could you repeat that?
10 Excuse me, could you help me, please?

LANGUAGE AND CULTURE

When someone says *Sorry* to you, you should try to make them feel better by answering: *It's okay. / It doesn't matter. / No problem*. And remember to smile! In Australia, people will often use the phrase *No worries* or *He/She'll be right, mate* when you say *Sorry* or *Thank you*. When you hear conversations in different English-speaking countries, don't be surprised if the accent – and some of the words – are different from standard English.

3 Mix and match

Welche Antwort ist richtig?

1 Sorry I'm late. ☐
2 Pardon? Could you repeat it, please? ☐
3 Excuse me, could you help me, please? ☐
4 Excuse me, could you tell me the way to the station, please? ☐

a Sorry, I'm afraid I'm a stranger here, too.
b Of course. What can I do for you?
c It's okay. Don't worry.
d Yes, sure – and I'll speak a bit more slowly.

4 Colours and clothes

bule aenjs: *blue jeans*

bakcl troeussr: ....

grnee jaectk: ....

bieeg situ: ....

ylloew bleosu: ....

rde desrs: ....

brnow pvuloler: ....

wthie shrtti: ....

5 Whose is it?

Complete the table.

I have a ticket.	It's my ticket.	It's mine.
.... have a ticket.	It's .... ticket.	It's yours.
.... has a ticket.	It's .... ticket.	It's his.
She has a ticket.	It's .... ticket.	It's ....
.... have a ticket.	It's our ticket.	It's ....
.... have a ticket.	It's their ticket.	It's ....

6 Katy's family

Liz and Rolf have two children – Robin and Katy. Robin is Katy's brother. He's married and has two children, Barbara and Ben.

Bilden Sie Sätze nach folgendem Muster:
Liz / Katy: *Liz is Katy's mother.*

1 Liz / Rolf ....

2 Barbara / Ben ....

3 Rolf / Robin ....

4 Barbara / Liz ....

5 Katy / Ben ....

6 Ben / Katy ....

7 A telephone conversation

Bringen Sie die Wörter in die richtige Reihenfolge.

1 Hello/Katy/is/this

....

2 I/to/speak/Could/please/Dad

.... ?

3 on/Hold/please/moment/a

....

4 the/code/What's/dialling/Austria/for/please

.... ?

8 Correct the sentences

Korrigieren Sie die Sätze.

1 Paul is the son of my friend.

....

2 I packed a blue jeans and a green pullover.

....

3 Whose is this camera? It isn't mines.

....

4 Hello, waiter – could we have the bill, please?

....

5 Hello, here is Pam. Can I speak to Jo, please?

....

6 Who is my key – can you see it?

....

p. 84

TOURIST TIP

Katy and Sam were lucky – their case *was* on the next flight! Make sure you know what to do if you lose important papers or if something is stolen. Before you go on holiday, write down the number of your passport and your driving licence and the phone numbers of your credit cards / mobile phone cancellation services. And make a photocopy of your important documents.

UNIT 6
DINING OUT

1 Starter

Choose a country and your teacher will write the name of that country on the board, e.g. *K-E-N-Y-A*. See how many items of food you can think of beginning with those letters: *kiwi, eggs, nuts* ...

2 19 At the restaurant

Katy and Sam are having a meal with two colleagues – Padma and Klaus.

Padma: I'm glad we reserved a table by the window – you get a great view from here.

Katy: Yes, it's lovely. Do you think it'll be nice weather tomorrow, too? I'm really looking forward to the Bridge Climb.

Klaus: The forecast is for sunshine all day – so it'll be hot up on the bridge. Don't forget your sun block ...

Waiter: So, here are the drinks – two dry white wines, a Foster's lager and a coke. Are you ready to order your food yet?

Sam: Yes, I think so. Padma, do you know what you want?

Padma: Yes, I'll have the prawn cocktail to start with, and I think I'll try the ostrich curry. That sounds ... interesting. And it comes with rice or chips. Hmmm – that's not a difficult choice – rice please.

Waiter: And you can choose boiled rice or vegetable pilau.

Padma: Just boiled rice, please.

Waiter: And for you, sir?

Klaus: The same starter for me, please, prawn cocktail. And, as a main course ... could I see the menu again? What exactly *is* "ostrich", Katy?

Katy: It's "*Strauss*" in German.

Klaus: Strauss!! Oh well, I'll try it! I'd like the ostrich curry with ... vegetable pilau rice.

Sam: Okay, my turn? Right, I'll have a bush salad followed by the kangaroo steak in red wine sauce with fresh vegetables and roast potatoes, please.

Katy: Oh, Sam! How could you eat kangaroo? Poor thing! I think I'll have the Bondi Beach seafood salad as a main course. And what's the soup of the day?

Waiter: Minestrone.

Katy: That's fine, thanks. As long as there's no meat in it ... . We'll order desserts later. And do you think we could have some more bread rolls? They were delicious!

Waiter: No worries. I'll be right back ... .

3 International cuisine

Match each dish with the correct description and the country it comes from.

Ostrich Curry	A soup made with mixed vegetables and noodles
Minestrone	Cold rice served with raw fish
Waldorf salad	Bacon, eggs and sausages served with tomatoes and mushrooms
Sushi	Lamb cooked with aubergines, tomatoes and cheese sauce
Full cooked breakfast	A salad made with celery, apples, walnuts, and mayonnaise
Moussaka	Ostrich meat cooked in a spicy sauce served with rice

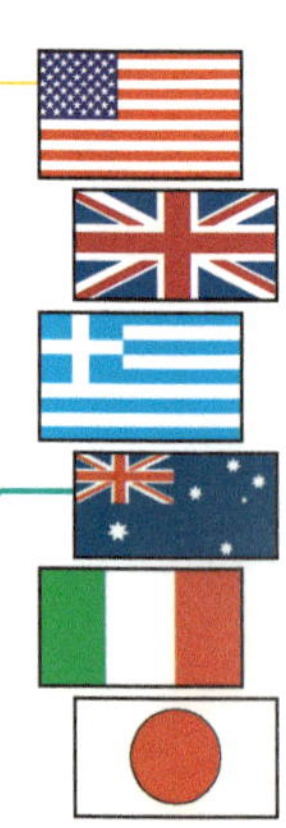

4 Placing your order

Work with a partner. Use the information in Activity 3 to ask about the dishes. Then order one of them, like this.

A: *What's sushi exactly?*
B: *It's cold rice served with raw fish.*
A: *Hmm, sounds delicious! I'll try the sushi.*

> **Remember:** Use *'ll (will)* to make spontaneous decisions: *I think I'll try the ostrich curry.*

5 A difficult customer

Complete these complaints. Put the numbers in the boxes.

☐ ... bread rolls aren't very fresh.
☐ ... think there's a mistake in the bill.
☐ ... that isn't what I ordered.
☐ ... glass is dirty.

Now decide what the waiter answers. Write the number of the complaint in the box:

☐ a Actually, it is correct, sir – there's a 15% service charge added.
☐ b Oh dear. Sorry. I'll bring you a clean one.
☐ c Oh, sorry. I'll bring you some fresh ones.
☐ d I'm very sorry, sir. My mistake. What did you order?

6 Where will she be next week?

Work in small groups. Look at the airport signs and discuss which city you think the flight attendant will be in next week:
I think she'll be in Edinburgh on Monday. / No, she won't – she'll be in London. Then write the city under the name of the airport.

> **Remember:** Use *'ll (will)* and *won't (will not)* to make predictions.

1 Tuesday: **J. F. KENNEDY INT.**

....

3 Thursday: **CHARLES DE GAULLE**

....

2 Wednesday: **HEATHROW**

....

4 Saturday: **TEGEL**

....

7 20 Weather report

Listen and write the name of the city next to the matching weather sign.

 ....  ....

 ....  ....

 ....  ....

Now with a partner, check your answers:
A: *What will the weather be like in London?*
B: *The forecast says it'll be ... / there'll be ... (foggy/fog) in (London).*

8 The restaurant game

Look at page 80. In pairs or groups of three, play the restaurant game and practise the phrases you learnt in this unit.

Now look at the Language Focus on page 46 of Pocket Tourist.

UNIT 6

DINING OUT

SELFSTUDY

In Unit 6 haben Sie gelernt wie man: • über das Wetter spricht • eine Mahlzeit in einem Restaurant bestellt • eine Beschwerde macht und das • *Future simple* mit *'ll (will)* und *won't (will not)* für Vorhersagen und spontane Entscheidungen verwendet. Üben Sie nun was Sie gelernt haben.

Desert

Rain forest

1 Australia – land of extremes

Ergänzen Sie folgende Wörter : *milder / rain / seasons / snows / storms / summer / sunshine / temperatures / tropical / weather / winds.*

When you think of Australia, you probably think of desert, sun and high (1) .... This is true of the centre of Australia, where it sometimes doesn't (2) .... for months! But even in the desert there can be (3) .... with heavy rain, thunder and lightning and strong (4) .... Because there are lots of different kinds of (5) .... conditions in Australia, there are lots of kinds of landscape. There are areas of (6) .... rain forests; wine-producing areas where the climate is (7) ....; and mountain areas where it (8) .... and people can go skiing in winter. And remember – the (9) .... in Australia are not at the same time of year as in Europe – winter is from June to August and (10) .... is from December to February, so Australians often eat their Christmas dinner on the beach in wonderful (11) ....!

2 21 Listen and repeat

Sprechen Sie die Sätze nach.

1 Could I see the menu, please?
2 What's the soup of the day?
3 I think I'll have a salad.
4 I'd like the steak, please.
5 I'm afraid this isn't very fresh.
6 Excuse me, but I think there's a mistake in the bill.
7 I'm sorry, but that isn't what I ordered.
8 Do you think we could have some more bread rolls?
9 What will the weather be like?
10 I think it'll be sunny tomorrow.

LANGUAGE AND CULTURE

In Australia you'll often see BYO restaurants – Bring Your Own. This means that the restaurant is not licensed to serve alcohol (Australian: booze), but if you pay a small 'corkage' charge[1], you can bring a bottle of wine you bought somewhere else – maybe at the local Bottle Shop. So you can choose your own wine and your own price.

1 corkage charge: Entkorkungsgebühr

3 How to order

Streichen Sie die falschen Wörter.

1 I'd like to *see / order* the menu, please.
2 Could I have a *glass wine / glass of wine*, please?
3 *Excuse me. / Hello.* Could we order now, please?
4 *I'd like / I like* a mixed salad, please.
5 *I have / I'll have* a steak with a baked potato, please.
6 I'll *pay / pay for* the meal.

"I'm 59 and she's 64. You call that fresh?"

4 I'm sorry but ...

1 (raw)

I'm sorry but these potatoes are raw.

2 (dirty)

I'm sorry but this ....

....

3 (cold)

....

....

4 (fresh)

....

....

5 (wrong)

....

....

5 Be spontaneous!

Ordnen Sie die spontane Reaktion rechts der passenden Situation links zu.

1 My camera is broken.	☐	a I'll help you.
2 It's cold in here.	☐	b I'll try to repair it.
3 I can't lift my case.	☐	c I'll answer it.
4 The telephone is ringing.	☐	d I'll close the window.

6 Predictions

Wohin werden Katy und Sam nächstes Jahr in Urlaub fahren? Was glauben Sie? Benutzen Sie *will ('ll)* für Ihre Antwort

a *Sam often has conferences in London so I'm sure they won't go to London on holiday.*

b *They love French food so I think* ....

....

....

c *Katy can speak some Russian so maybe* ....

....

....

d *I know!* ....

....

....

p. 84

TOURIST TIP

Tipping in restaurants in Australia is not normally expected – only, perhaps, for extremely good service or in the best restaurants. Make sure you know what the custom is in your host country – who to tip (taxi drivers, waiters, hairdressers) and how much to tip!

UNIT 7

BRIDGE CLIMB

Auckland

San Francisco

1 Starter

Tell the class one city you have been to and one city you have never been to but you would like to go to:
I've been to (Auckland) but I've never been to (San Francisco). I'd really like to go there.

2 22 Safety first

One of Sydney's tourist attractions is the beautiful Sydney Harbour Bridge. And, if you're fit enough, you can climb the bridge! That's what Katy and Sam have decided to do.

Katy: I'm a bit nervous about this. How do you feel, Sam? Have you ever done anything like this before?
Sam: Well, I've climbed to the top of the Statue of Liberty, if you count that. But this will be much more exciting!
Katy: Yes. Well, first we have to fill in this health questionnaire.
Sam: I'll do yours at the same time as mine, okay? You can get the camera ready – but don't drop it! We don't want any more accidents with my brother's camera.
Katy: Okay, read out the questions.
Sam: Right, number one. Are you taller than one metre fifty?
Katy: Yes, of course I am. Now just ask me the questions you don't know the answers to.
Sam: Have you ever suffered from serious headaches?
Katy: No. Well, I occasionally get headaches when you talk about sports cars!
Sam: ... or epilepsy?
Katy: No.
Sam: Have you ever suffered from heart problems?
Katy: No.
Sam: Have you ever had an AIDS test?
Katy: Why do they want to know that?
Sam: Probably just in case you have an accident.
Katy: Well, yes, I have actually. I had an AIDS test two years ago.
Sam: And ...?
Katy: Sam!
Sam: All right! Next question: Are you pregnant?
Katy: Sam!!!
Sam: Okay, okay, just checking!
Katy: Here, give me that form. I think I'll fill it in myself. But I have to go to the loo first – I've got a funny feeling in my stomach.

3 Questions and answers

Give short answers to these questions.

1 Does Katy feel nervous?
2 Has Sam ever been to America?
3 Do they have to fill in a questionnaire?
4 Is the camera theirs?
5 Has Katy ever suffered from heart problems?
6 Did she have an AIDS test last year?

4 23 Sydney Harbour Bridge

Before the climb, the guide gave the group some information about the Bridge Climb. Write down the numbers you hear.

1 ....°C	6 .... cm
2 .... m high	7 .... hrs
3 .... yrs	8 .... a.m.
4 19..........	9 .... mins
5 .... m long	10 Au$ ....

Listen again and then tell the class a piece of information about one of the statistics you have written down.

5 Have you ever ... ?

Work with a partner. Take it in turns to ask and answer these questions. Fill in the table with a tick or a cross. Only answer with *Yes, I have* (✓) or *No, I haven't* (✗).

Have you ever ...?

1 ... ridden a motorbike?	☐
2 ... missed your flight?	☐
3 ... talked to a famous person?	☐
4 ... visited an English-speaking country?	☐
5 ... smuggled?	☐
6 ... stolen from a shop?	☐

6 Tell us about it!

Look at exercise 5 again. Write down two things about your partner (one ✗ and one ✓) on a piece of paper, e.g. *Uwe has never smuggled but he has stolen from a shop*, and give it to your teacher.

Your teacher will now read out the sentence – but not the name – from one piece of paper. Guess who the person is and find out more information by asking questions beginning with: *Where did ...? How did ... ? What did ...? Did you ...? When did ...? Was ...? Were ...?*

e.g. A: *What did you steal?*
Uwe: *I stole an ice-cream.*

> **Remember:** Use the *present perfect* to tell people about an experience you had at some time in your life; use the *past simple* to give details about this experience.

7 How often?

Put these words in order of frequency by matching them with the frequency symbols.

often	✓✓✓✓✓✓✓
never	✓✓✓✓✓
usually	✓✓✓✓
rarely	✓✓✓
sometimes	✓
always	✗

(often — ✓✓✓✓)

8 Sam and Katy's holiday routine

Look at the table below and make sentences about Sam and Katy's daily routine like this: *Sam always gets up at 6.30 a.m.*

> **Remember:** The "how often" adverbs go before the main verb: I occasionally send postcards.

	Sam	Katy
get up at 6.30 a.m.	✓✓✓✓✓✓✓	✗
drink a cup of coffee	✓✓✓	✓✓✓✓✓✓✓
eat an English breakfast	✓✓✓✓✓	✓
read the morning newspaper	✗	✓✓✓
go for a swim in the hotel pool	✓✓✓✓	✓✓✓✓

9 How often do you do that?

Ask people in the class how often they do some of these things – and why, e.g. *I (never) phone home when I go on holiday because (my family is with me).*

How often do you ...

• stay on a camp site • travel by plane • hire a car • go abroad • go sightseeing • sunbathe • speak English • phone home • stay in a hotel • eat the local food • eat in restaurants • pack too many clothes • take photographs • use traveller's cheques • use a credit card ... when you go on holiday?

Now look at the Language Focus on page 47 of Pocket Tourist.

UNIT 7
BRIDGE CLIMB

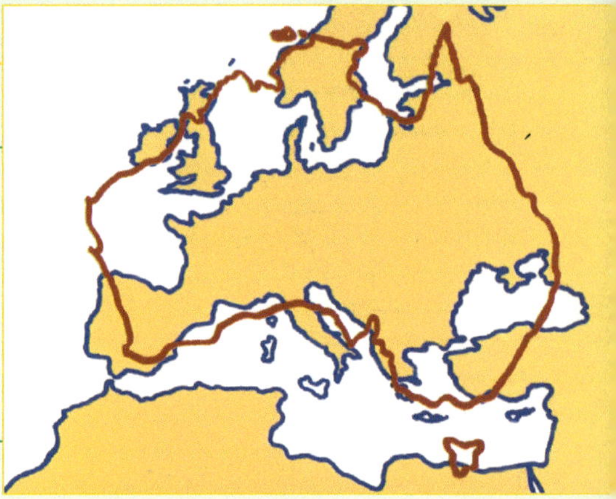

SELFSTUDY

Unit 7 haben Sie gelernt wie man: • Statistiken versteht • mit dem *present perfect* ausdrückt, ob man etwas schon einmal gemacht hat • mit dem *past tense* Details von Ereignissen in der Vergangenheit angibt und • Angaben zur Häufigkeit macht. Üben Sie nun, was Sie gelernt haben.

1 Is that a fact?

Setzen Sie folgende Zahlen in den Text ein.

120° / 30 / 40% / 250 / 19,000,000 / 13,000

Australia is (1) .... miles (20,900 km) away from Britain.

It is more than (2) .... times bigger than the United Kingdom but the population of Australia is much smaller – (3) ...., compared with Britain's fifty-nine million.

(4) .... of Australians have one parent born abroad and only 2 percent of Australians have Aborigine blood. Of course it's a very hot country – the highest temperature recorded was forty-nine point two degrees Celsius, that's (5) .... Fahrenheit, in Western Australia. But some towns in North Queensland have (6) .... inches (635 cm) of rain a year – that's as high as a double-decker bus!

Schreiben Sie nun die Zahlen in Worten.

LANGUAGE AND CULTURE

Katy is nervous before the climb and has to go to the toilet. She asks the guide: *"Excuse me, where's the loo, please?"*. An American would ask: *"Where's the bathroom, please?"*.
In public buildings like restaurants and theatres you usually see the sign *Ladies* and *Gents* (BE) or *Restroom* (AE) on the lavatory doors. And on the street you may see the sign *Public Convenience*.

2 24 Listen and repeat

Sprechen Sie die Sätze nach.

1 How do you feel?
2 Have you ever done anything like this before?
3 I've never been to Australia.
4 I'd really like to go there.
5 I've been to London.
6 I was there in 1999.
7 How often do you have a holiday abroad?
8 We sometimes have an English breakfast.
9 The temperature was thirty-two degrees.
10 It's about two hundred and fifty kilometres away.

3 What have they done?

Setzen Sie die Verben in das *present perfect (has/have done)*.

1 Sam (climb) .... the Statue of Liberty.
2 Katy (do) .... never .... anything like that.
3 She (take) .... lots of photos.
4 (eat) .... you ever .... Japanese food?
5 I (not meet) .... Katy's mother.

shark: Hai

4 Make questions

Bilden Sie Fragesätze und wählen Sie dabei die richtige Verbform.

1 they / *drink, drank, drunk* / Australian / Have / ever / beer

....

.... ?

2 Did / waiter / tip / *give, gave, given* / you / a / the / dinner / after

.... ?

3 did / plane / What / *take, took, taken* / time / the / off

.... ?

4 ever / Has / *eat, ate, eaten* / he / ostrich

.... ?

5 you / American / an / *speak, spoke, spoken* / Have / ever / to

.... ?

6 *swim, swam, swum* / sea / in / Did / the / you / year / last

.... ?

5 Choose the right tense

Welche Zeitform ist richtig: *present perfect (have/has done)* oder *simple past (did)*?

1 (see) .... you ever .... a crocodile?

2 No, I (see) .... never .... a crocodile but I (see) .... an alligator. I (see) .... one when I (go) .... to South Africa in 1999.

3 I (fly) .... never .... in a helicopter. (do) .... you ever .... that?

4 Not me! My brother (fly) .... in a helicopter! And he (fly) .... in a sports plane, too. He (fly) .... over the Grand Canyon in America last year.

TOURIST TIP

It is sometimes difficult to understand English native speakers if they have a dialect or if they speak too fast. And in countries where English is the *lingua franca*, people you speak to may have a strong accent. So learn a few phrases for situations when you don't understand what people say to you: *Sorry, I don't understand. / Could you speak slowly, please? / Could you say that again, please? / Is there anybody here who speaks German?* And take Pocket Tourist with you on holiday to give you more help.

6 25 Speaking English

Padma und Katy sprechen über ihre Familien.

Hören Sie den Dialog an und ergänzen Sie die fehlenden Informationen:

1 Katy's mother .... English to her.

2 Katy's father .... English at home.

3 Katy's father .... English at work.

4 Padma and her family .... Hindi at home.

5 Padma and her family .... English when they have guests.

p. 85

UNIT 8

UP, UP AND AWAY

1 Starter

Fill in the four car stickers with the international letters for four different countries and write the name of each country on the lines. Then ask other members of the class:

Where is (GB) from?

(GB) is from (Great Britain).

( ) ....

( ) ....

( ) ....

( ) ....

Remember: If you need help with the alphabet, look at page 63 of Pocket Tourist.

Car Rental Sydney Australia offers car hire discounts on new cars - Microsoft Internet Explorer

Adresse http://www.discountcar.com.au/bookingform.htm

Main
Booking Form
Fleet/Rates
Terms
Tourism
Franchises
Locations

Car Rental value in Australia

Australia Car Rentals Discounts
Head Office:
204 Oxford Street,
Bondi Junction
Australia, 2025

Discount Car & Truck Rentals
Canada & USA
www.discountcar.com

Designed by Web Site Marketing and Design

Best Viewed @800X600 using Internet Explorer or Netscape Navigator version 4.0 or up

Useful Links:
- Street Directory
- Sports
- Airport Buses

Booking Form

Discount CAR AND TRUCK RENTALS

Reservation Requests

Please complete the following form if you would like to request a reservation with our company:

First name
Last name
Country or State (if Australia)
Phone number
E-mail
(Correct address is required to reply back)
Age 25 or over
Select vehicle Select vehicle
Click arrow above for dropdown menu and car selection.
Select Area of use
PARRA
Baby Sea
Pickup lo
Sydney
Internatio

2 26 Renting a car

Sam: Look, Katy – I've found a cheaper one. I've looked at five car rental websites and this company is the cheapest I can find – and it has a better selection of cars, too.

Katy: Okay. You know I don't really like the idea of driving a hired car. But I suppose hiring a car is the only way we can get to the Blue Mountains in time for our balloon flight.

Sam: Yes, it is. I'll complete the form so that you can drive too. Did you bring your driving licence with you?

Katy: Yes, of course I did. But don't hire anything too expensive – or anything that uses lots of petrol.

Sam: How about this? In price group A you can have a weekend special – three days for the price of two costs only 120 Australian dollars.

Katy: What if we have an accident? Are we insured?

Sam: The price includes insurance for any accidents, but we would have to pay the first 100 dollars.

Katy: And there's no limit to the number of miles we're allowed to do?

Sam: No, it's unlimited mileage. And we don't have to hand back the keys until Monday morning.

Katy: So, the only extra is the fuel.

Sam: Yes. Right, let's book one of these then, okay? 'Area of use' – how do you spell Parramatta?

Katy: P – A – double R – A –M – A – double T – A.

Sam: No baby seat needed. 'Select vehicle' – what do you fancy, a Daihatsu Charade or a Suzuki Swift?

Katy: Oh, why don't you choose? You're the expert on cars. Just book one that doesn't go bung.

Sam: What?

Katy: Just book one that doesn't break down. *Go bung* – that's Australian for break down ...

3 Say it another way

Read the text to find a different way of saying these sentences by changing only the underlined words.

1 It has a better choice of cars.
2 I'll fill in the form.
3 Don't rent anything too expensive.
4 We don't have to give back the keys until Monday morning.
5 The only extra cost is the petrol.
6 What would you like?

4 Form-filling

The language on forms is sometimes complicated. Match the questions with the headings you might see on a form:

1 Surname	☐	a Where do you live?
2 Place of birth	☐	b What's your job?
3 Permanent address	☐	c Are you married or single?
4 Occupation	☐	d What's your family name?
5 Marital status	☐	e Where were you born?

Now work with a partner. Ask him / her these questions and write down the answers. You might need to ask: *Could you spell that, please?*

5 In other words

The English you hear abroad may be American or British English. In some countries they use the words *petrol, motorways and lorries* (BE) and in other places they say *gas, highways and trucks* (AE). In Australia they often shorten words. Can you guess what these Australian words mean?

a roo	breakfast
b vegies	afternoon
c breckie	crocodile
d croc	barbecue
e barbie	kangaroo
f arvo	vegetables

6 Problems

Remember: Use the *present perfect* when you can see the result of a completed action: e.g.: *I've done my homework.*

Replace the word in italics with two other possible items.

Oh no, I've lost my *credit card.*

....

Oh no, I've broken my *tooth.*

....

Oh no, I've forgotten my *map.*

....

Now work with a partner. In turns tell your partner your problems. He/She will make helpful suggestions: *You should ... / You could ... / Why don't you ...?*

7 27 Dictation

Listen and write down the letters to spell the name of an Australian city. _ _ _ _ _ _ _ _ _

Here are some words to help you: *in / on / under / next to / opposite / between / in front of / behind / below / above / on the left / on the right.*

Now write down the name of a city you'd like to visit. Dictate it to a partner in the same way as on the cassette/CD.

8 28 A bird's-eye view

Katy and Sam are looking down from the hot-air balloon. They can see the town below them.

Your teacher will divide the class into two groups, A and B. A students, please turn to page 77 and look at the town below the balloon. B students, please turn on page 79 and look at the town below the balloon.

Now look at the Language Focus on page 48 of Pocket Tourist.

UNIT 8

UP, UP AND AWAY

SELFSTUDY

Unit 8 haben Sie gelernt wie man: • mit dem *present perfect* das Ergebnis einer Handlung ausdrückt • Ratschläge gibt und Vorschläge macht • Ortsangaben macht und • ein Formular ausfüllt. Üben Sie nun, was Sie gelernt haben.

Ayers Rock

1 Ayers Rock

Setzen Sie die Verben in das *present perfect*.

(1 hear) .... you ever .... of Uluru? Maybe you (2 not hear) .... the name before, but most people (3 see) .... pictures of it. Uluru is the original, *Aboriginal*, name for Ayers Rock, the most spectacular monolith in the world. It is 100 million years old and is 335 metres high, 3.6 kilometres long and 25 kilometres wide. When Ernest Gosse discovered it in 1872, he named it Ayers Rock after Sir Henry Ayers, the South Australian Prime Minister of the day. Since then the Rock (4 become) .... one of Australia's major tourist attractions. In the 1960s, there were 10,000 visitors a year, but now there are about 1,000 every day. Because there are now so many visitors, the local people (5 build) .... an airport nearby and (6 develop) .... a large tourist centre, the Ayers Rock Resort. In 1985 the Australian government gave back the Rock to the Anangu Aboriginal people. To these Aborigines, Uluru is a sacred place and so they (7 try) .... to limit the number of tourists (they call them *minga* – ants[1]). You can climb to the top of the Rock, but the path is closed on very hot days because there (8 be) .... lots of accidents. Some tourists (9 die) .... of sunstroke and others (10 have) .... heart attacks, so now there are very tough safety regulations before visitors are allowed to climb the Rock.

1 ants: Ameisen

LANGUAGE AND CULTURE

In many countries, the number plate of a car tells you which part of the country the car is from. But in some countries drivers can choose a number plate which spells their name or tells you something about their job or personality. Some newspapers advertise these number plates. Who or what sort of person do you think these number plates might belong to?

JB 007	E1 TON	B G8S
P1 LOT	MPH 200	WE R4

p. 85

2 29 Listen and repeat

Sprechen Sie die Sätze nach.

1 I'll fill in the form.
2 How do you spell it?
3 Are we insured?
4 What do you fancy?
5 Why don't you choose?
6 Are you married or single?
7 I've lost my credit card.
8 I've broken my tooth.
9 You should go to the dentist's.
10 It's opposite the bank.

3 Fill in the form

Ergänzen Sie im Formular folgende Stichwörter:
Surname / Place of birth / Date of birth / Nationality / Phone number / Address / Sex / Signature / Occupation / First name

1	....	WITSCHAS
2	....	KLAUS
3	....	☑ male ☐ female
4	....	14/11/75
5	....	LINZ, AUSTRIA
6	....	AUSTRIAN
7	....	RADIOLOGIST
8	....	Seefeldstr. 340, 8008 Zurich, CH
9	....	01-2613675
10	....	*Klaus Witschas*

5 Why don't you...?

Sehen Sie sich die Einkaufsstraße unten an und vervollständigen Sie die Vorschläge.

1 "Someone has stolen my handbag." "You *should* go to the *police station*. Look, it's there, *opposite* the post office."

2 "I'm really hungry. I haven't had any breakfast." "Why _ _ _' _ you go to the ....? Look, it's there, _ _ _ _ _ _ _ the police station and the bank."

3 "I think I've broken a tooth – it's very painful." "You _ _ _ _ _ _ go to the .... Look, it's there, _ _ _ _ _ the newsagent's."

4 "I haven't posted our postcards yet – I haven't got any stamps." "_ _ _ don't you go to the ....? Look it's there, on the _ _ _ _ _ of the newsagent's."

4 30 Could you spell that for me?

In Australien gibt es viele ungewöhnliche Ortsbezeichnungen. Hören Sie zu und notieren Sie die Namen.

1 ....
2 ....
3 ....
4 ....

p. 85

TOURIST TIP

The cost of hiring a car can be very different from one country to another – and so can driving customs. In many countries in South East Asia and the Pacific (including Australia and Japan) you must drive on the left. If you plan to hire a car, it's a good idea to find out about rules of the road, speed limits, wearing seat belts, fuel prices, motorway tolls[1] etc. before you leave home. To hire a car, you need a valid[2] driving licence and you'll have to pay a deposit[3].

1 tolls: Gebühren, 2 valid: gültig, 3 deposit: die Kaution

SOUTH AFRICAN HIGHLIGHTS
SOUTH AFRICAN HIGHLIGHTS

Have you ever been to South Africa? If you have, tell the class about some of your experiences.

THE RAINBOW NATION

When he became the president of South Africa in April 1994, Nelson Mandela called his 42 million people the 'Rainbow Nation' because of the colourful multi-racial mix. The Bantu is the country's largest population group with over 30 million people. But over the last three hundred years, people have come from all over the world to work in South Africa. British and Dutch settlers established trading companies on the Cape; the Chinese came to work in the gold and diamond mines; and many Indians originally came to work on the sugar plantations. Even today, Durban has the largest population of Indians living outside India.

People with the South African flag painted on their faces.

LEADER – OF FASHION?

Nelson Mandela was born in 1918 and, as a young man, he was already politically active and became the leader of the ANC (African National Congress). In 1964 the South African government sent him to prison for life because of his political activities. He was freed in 1990 and, in 1994 – a year after he received the Nobel Peace Prize – he became South Africa's first black president. Everyone has heard of Nelson Mandela – but did you know he became a fashion icon when he was in his 70s? Mandela started a trend in clothes with his colourful, silk shirts. On the Waterfront in Cape Town there's a famous shop called *The President's Shirt*, where you can buy these "Mandela shirts".

ROBBEN ISLAND

The Dutch settlers gave this island its name because so many seals[1] lived there. But it's famous because it's where Nelson Mandela spent eighteen years of his twenty-six year prison term (1964-1990). In 1996, the last prisoner left Robben Island and it became a National Monument. Today the prison is a museum which tells the story of South Africa's fight for independence. Many of the tour guides are ex-prisoners or guards and have their own personal stories to tell. 300 tourists a day are allowed to make the 45 minute ferry trip from Cape Town's harbour to the island, where they can learn about South African history and also see some wonderful examples of South African wildlife.

1 seal: Robbe

Robben Island, South Africa

TABLE MOUNTAIN

One of the most impressive sights in South Africa is the breathtaking Table Mountain – Cape Town's unforgettable landmark. It's 1087 metres high and, if you're fit, you can choose one of the 300 routes to climb it (but, for the less energetic, a six minute ride in a cable car will get you to the top!). Local people speak of the Tablecloth[1] when the top of the mountain is covered with thick, white clouds. Cape Town, South Africa's second largest city, is the one which attracts the most foreign tourists – about 750,000 a year.

1 tablecloth: Tischtuch

DIAMONDS ARE FOREVER

Much of South Africa's wealth comes from its diamond industry. The first diamonds were discovered there in 1867 and soon speculators arrived from all over Africa and Europe. At first, the diamond industry was controlled by a few well-paid (mostly white) experts who employed large numbers of badly-paid black workers. Stealing soon became a problem. To stop this, the companies built camps for the black workers. They had to live there and guards searched them when they finished work. This was the start of a two-class system – later called *apartheid* – which continued in South Africa for the next 100 years.

LANGUAGE CORNER

There are many different tribal languages in South Africa but there are two official languages: Afrikaans, which is similar to Dutch, and English. English is the first language of only about 10% of the people in South Africa but most people speak it as a second language. Read this postcard and see if you can find the standard English words for the South African words.

English words:
a truck, b men/guys, c very soon, d great, e alcohol, f traffic lights, g barbecue, h liquor store,

Hi Peter,
We're having a lekker (1) .... time here in Cape Town. Yesterday we had a braai (2) .... with a few friends. First we went to the bottle store (3) .... in Jay's bakkie (4) .... and we had a crash at the robots (5) .... ! (Luckily this was before we drank any dopp (6) .... so there were no problems with the police!) Must go - Pam will be here now-now (7) .... and we want to visit a safari park this afternoon.
Regards to all the okes (8) .... at work,
James.

p. 84

SOUTH AFRICAN HIGHLIGHTS
SPOTLIGHT ON WILDLIFE

Lion

Nine out of ten tourists go to South Africa to see the wildlife – not only the Big Five: lions, elephants, rhinos, buffalo and leopards – but also zebras, giraffes, crocodiles, baboons, hippos and deer. At one time people went on safaris to hunt the animals – now most people go on safaris to *look* at the animals, not to kill them.

Rhinos

TRANSFRONTIER PEACE PARKS

Elephant

Have you heard about Peace Parks? These transfrontier conservation areas were the idea of a South African businessman, Dr. Anton Rupert. His plan was to enlarge the Kruger National Park in South Africa with the help of the neighbouring countries of Mozambique and Zimbabwe. In the year 2000, the 100,000 km^2 Great Limpopo Transfrontier Conservation Area was opened – a nature paradise the size of Portugal.

ADDO ELEPHANT NATIONAL PARK

In the early 1900s, there were 10,000,000 elephants in the whole of Africa. Today there are only 600,000. People hunted elephants for their ivory tusks – one tusk could weigh between 30 and 45 kilos! And farmers killed elephants because they ate the vegetation – elephants need about 300 kilos of food each day. Now most of the elephants enjoy life in game reservations and National Parks like the Addo Elephant National Park near Port Elizabeth – but tourists are often warned not to take any fruit with them or they will get a closer look at an elephant than is comfortable!

Springbok

THE SPRINGBOK

The country's national emblem is the springbok – this is just one of the many species of antelope in South Africa. It's called a springbok because it can jump more than ten metres in the air when it's attacked. This warns other springbok of the danger – and also puzzles its attacker. The South African rugby team – the Springboks – is named after this animal.

BIRDS

There are over 500 different species of birds in South Africa and more than half of them have their home in the Kruger National Park. You can see all kinds of birds in South Africa – from pelicans to penguins. Ostriches are a popular attraction, too. Highgate Ostrich Farm near Oudtshoorn is one of the many places where you can see ostrich races – and, if you want to, you can be one of the jockeys. But, be careful: these large birds are not very clever – they have a brain the size of a chicken's; and they are dangerous – they can kill an adult with one kick; and they're fast – they can run at a speed of 80 km per hour!

Ostrich

THE DRAKENSBERG MOUNTAINS

Rock paintings in the Drakensberg mountains

The Drakensberg Mountain range is 1,000 km long and many of the mountains are over 3,000 m high. One quarter of all the animal species in South Africa can be found here. And you can see dinosaurs' footprints from 200 million years ago! There are also over 60,000 rock paintings, which were made by the San People, or Bushmen, one of the oldest racial groups in the world. An ideal place for an activity holiday – not only for watching wildlife but also for biking, climbing, trekking, horse-riding, fishing, sailing – and even for skiing in winter (from May to August).

Tail fin of a Gray Whale

WHALE WATCHING

On the West Cape there are over 40 different species of whale and some of them live to be 100 years old. They return to this area every year because it is their breeding ground and the young whales are born here in August. It's forbidden to get closer than 300 metres to a whale so that they are not disturbed in their home waters. Some of the whale stations have underwater microphones and whale watchers can hear the whales communicating with each other.

What attracts people to come to your country for a holiday?

PUZZLE CORNER

What can you remember?

1 The original inhabitants of the Drakensberg Mountains were
a) San People
b) Aborigines
c) Maoris

2 The Great Limpopo Transfrontier Conservation Area is in
a) South Africa, Mozambique, and Botswana
b) South Africa, Zambia and Botswana
c) South Africa, Mozambique, and Zimbabwe

3 The springbok is a type of
a) deer
b) zebra
c) antelope

4 Table Mountain overlooks
a) Durban
b) Cape Town
c) Pretoria

5 The Springboks are a South African
a) football team
b) rugby team
c) cricket team

p. 84

The Adventures of Ivor Problem and Annie Mergency

AT THE DOCTOR'S AND THE CHEMIST'S

Ivor ist im Urlaub und fühlt sich krank. Also macht er einen Termin mit dem ortsansässigen Arzt aus.

Wenn Sie die Geschichte lesen, aufschreiben oder nachspielen, können Sie die markierten Ausdrücke durch jeweils einen anderen Ausdruck in der gleichen Farbe ersetzen. Weitere nützliche Wörter und Redewendungen zum Thema Gesundheit und Krankheit finden Sie in Pocket Tourist auf den Seiten 33-36.

I'd like to, Can I	matter, trouble	cough, cold
this afternoon, later this morning	awful, dreadful	just opposite, over the road

twice, three times	travel sickness, hay fever	great, fine
these mosquito bites, this allergy	sleepy, dizzy	Pardon?, What did you say?

WELCOME TO HONG KONG

After spending a wonderful fortnight in and around Sydney, Katy and Sam stop off in Hong Kong for a holiday before returning home to the UK. They enjoy some of the sights and sounds of this colourful country. And they have some news to tell Liz and Rolf when they get home!

Hong Kong harbour

Market in the Western District of Hong Kong

Chinese New Year Parade

UNIT 9
XIANG GANG

1 Starter

Ask other students a question about the sights and facilities (entertainment, shops, ...) in their town.

Think of a question beginning with: *Excuse me, how (often / far / much / many / long / old) ...?* If someone asks you a question and you don't know the answer, say: *I'm sorry, I don't know. Let's ask (Klaus).*

2 Lei Garden Hotel

Look at the advert for the Lei Garden Hotel, where Katy and Sam are staying in Hong Kong (Chinese name: Xiang Gang). What does it tell you about the hotel?

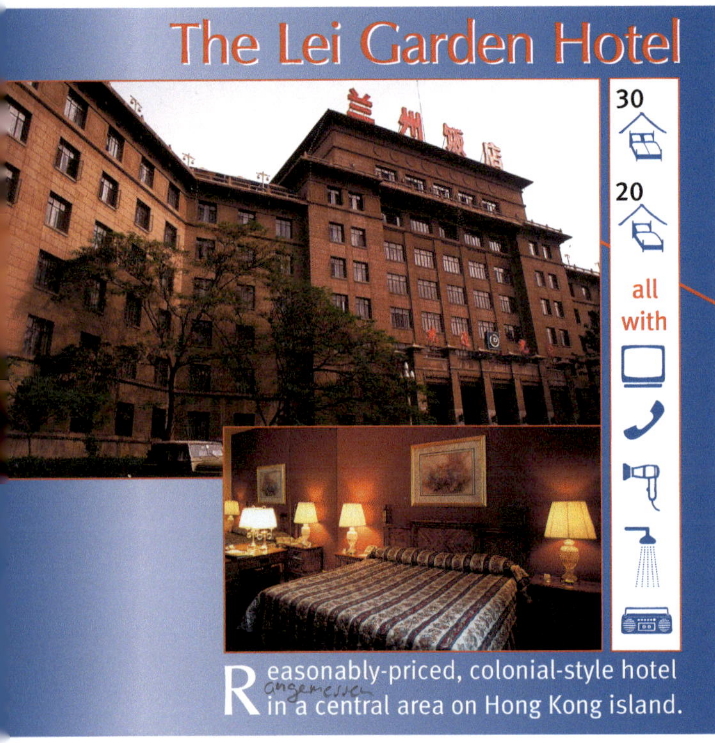

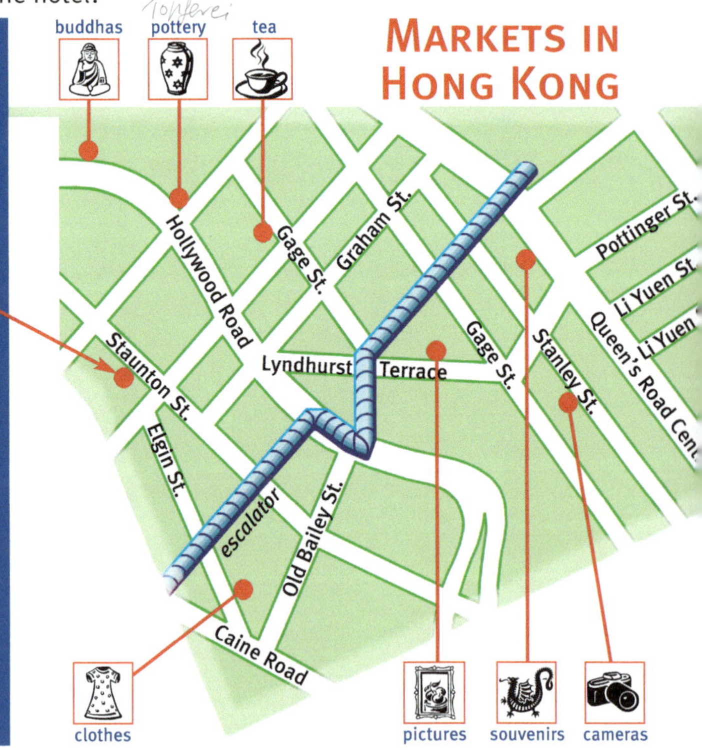

3 31 Booking a room

Listen to the phone call Sam made when he booked a room at the Lei Garden Hotel. Underline what he asked for:

1 Do you have a *single / double* room for *three / four* nights?
2 We'd like to check in on *Tuesday / Thursday* evening.
3 Does the room have *an en suite bathroom / a shower*?
4 We'd like *bed and breakfast / bed, breakfast and evening meal*.
5 Can we pay by *traveller's cheque / credit card*?

Remember: You can ask: *Do you have ...? / Does it have ...?* or *Have you got ...? / Has it got ...?*

Now ask questions 1 and 3 again and use *got* in the question.

4 Asking for information

Sam asked the receptionist for more information. Here are her answers. What questions did he ask?

1 No, I'm afraid there isn't a view of the sea.
2 Bed and breakfast costs 360 HK$ per person per night.
3 Breakfast is served from 7a.m. to 10.30 a.m.
4 Oh yes, all our staff speak English.
5 You can change money here in the hotel.
6 You can go to the town centre by tram or bus – or you can walk – it isn't far.
7 Yes, sir. The room has got a large balcony.

5 What would you say?

You're booking a room at a hotel. Write down what you would say. Then compare your sentences with a partner.

1 

2 

3 

4 

5 

6 Hotel rules

Work in small groups. Draw a line between phrases with similar meaning:

1 you must	you're allowed to
2 you needn't	you have to
3 you can	you aren't allowed to
4 you mustn't	you don't have to

Remember: You mustn't do it. = *Sie dürfen es nicht machen.* – You needn't do it. = *Sie brauchen es nicht zu machen.*

1 

2 

3 

Say where you might see these hotel signs. Make two sentences about each sign, using two of the above phrases.

Now talk about rules • where you work • where you live and • where you learn English.

7 Crossword Hotel

Work with a partner. Find the right words and fit them into the grid to form a new word – something you'll find in your hotel wardrobe. Remember you can use your dictionary, if necessary.

1 Nice to sit here in the sun (7).
2 You wash with this (4).
3, 4 You need both of these to make a bed (7, 6).
5, 6 Without this, the bathroom floor gets wet (6, 7).
7 A bedroom with a bathroom attached (2, 5).
8 Your hairdryer has got one, so has your travel iron – but you may need an adaptor (4).
9 Pick this up at the reception (3).
10 You can see yourself in it (6).

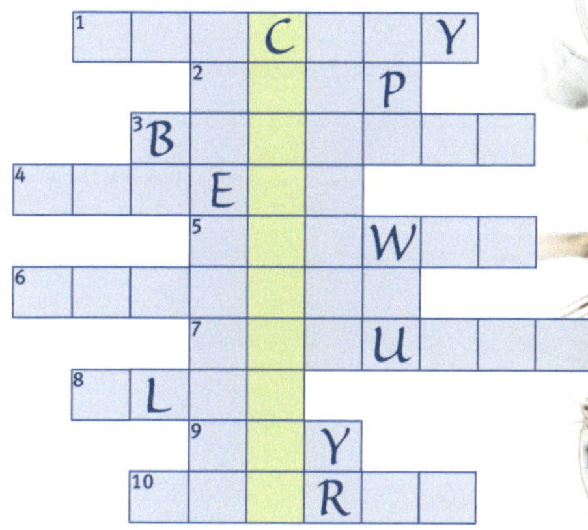

8 32 Asking the way

Katy and Sam want to visit a local market. The hotel receptionist tells them the way. Mark the route from the hotel to the market on the map of Hong Kong on the left.

Work with a partner. Each choose a market on the map that you'd like to go to – but don't tell your partner. Give directions from the hotel to the market and see if he / she can find it. Here are some phrases to help you: *Go straight on. Turn left / right. Take the first / second / third street on the left / right. Cross over. It's in front of... / opposite ... / near ... .*

9 Asking questions

Practise asking questions. Look at page 81.

10 Talk about it

In small groups, talk about the best / worst hotel you have stayed at. Say what you liked / didn't like about it.

Now look at the Language Focus on page 49 of Pocket Tourist.

UNIT 9
XIANG GANG

Peak Tram

SELFSTUDY

In Unit 9 haben Sie gelernt wie man: • nach Informationen fragt • ein Hotelzimmer bucht • einen Weg beschreibt, und • ausdrückt, ob man etwas tun darf oder muss. Üben Sie nun, was Sie gelernt haben.

1 Xiang Gang

Xiang Gang – 'fragrant harbour'[1] – is the Chinese name for Hong Kong. The main areas of Hong Kong are Kowloon, Lantau, the New Territories and the island of Hong Kong – and there are about 250 smaller islands. 95% of the 7,000,000 inhabitants of Hong Kong are Chinese but it was a British colony from 1841-1997. Each year 13 million tourists visit Hong Kong. Read about five of its biggest tourist attractions:

Feng Shui House

Ordnen Sie folgende Überschriften jeweils dem richtigen Text zu:

Victoria Peak – Star Ferry – Big Buddha – Ocean Park – Feng-Shui Tour

1 .... There's something for everybody in this spectacular theme park – Kids' World, Bird Paradise, Goldfish Garden, Film Fantasia – a day of fun for both adults and children.

2 .... This is the most beautiful – and cheapest – way to travel across Victoria harbour to Kowloon. Sail on this 100 year-old double-decker boat between the old wooden fishing boats and modern luxury liners.

3 .... Spend half a day learning more about the 3,000 year-old "teachings of wind and water". See how even the most modern buildings in Hong Kong were built to be at one with nature.

4 .... Leave Hong Kong island for the day and take an hour's boat trip to see this massive bronze statue (34 m. high) in the mountains of Lantau island.

5 .... A 'must' for all Hong- Kong visitors is the 8-minute ride on the Peak Tram to the highest point on Hong Kong island. Here you have a panoramic view of the harbour and futuristic skyline. The tram made its first 373-metre-high journey in 1888.

1 fragrant harbour: Der Hafen der Düfte

2 33 Listen and repeat

Sprechen Sie die Sätze nach.

1 Have you got a double room for three nights?
2 We'd like bed, breakfast and evening meal.
3 Does it have an en suite bathroom?
4 Can I change money at the hotel?
5 Excuse me, do you speak English?
6 Could you tell us how to get to the market?
7 How far is it to the town centre from here?
8 Do you know where the nearest bus stop is?
9 How often do the buses run?
10 Thank you very much for your help.

LANGUAGE AND CULTURE

In many countries English is the second language. In Hong Kong the official language is Cantonese but, because Hong Kong was a British colony for many years, English is spoken in most hotels and shops, and street names and roadsigns are usually in both languages. Outside the tourist areas, fewer people speak English. Hong Kong policemen who can speak English have a red flash[1] on the shoulder of their uniform.

1 red flash: roter Farbblitz

3 Say it in English

Ordnen Sie den deutschen Sätzen die richtigen Übersetzungen zu.

1 Das brauchen Sie nicht zu machen.	☐	a You mustn't do that.
2 Machen Sie das nicht.	☐	b You don't have to do that.
3 Das könnten Sie machen.	☐	c You have to do that.
4 Das dürfen Sie nicht machen.	☐	d You could do that.
5 Das können Sie nicht machen.	☐	e You should do that.
6 Das sollten Sie machen.	☐	f Why don't you do that?
7 Das müssen Sie machen.	☐	g You can't do that.
8 Warum machen Sie das nicht?	☐	h Don't do that.

4 34 A hotel reservation

Hören Sie sich das Telefongespräch an und füllen Sie das Formular aus.

Family Name: ....

Mr ☐ Ms ☐

Single room ☐ Double room ☐

Number of nights: ....

From: .... To: ....

Special requirements: ....

....

Credit card number: ....

5 Leaving a message

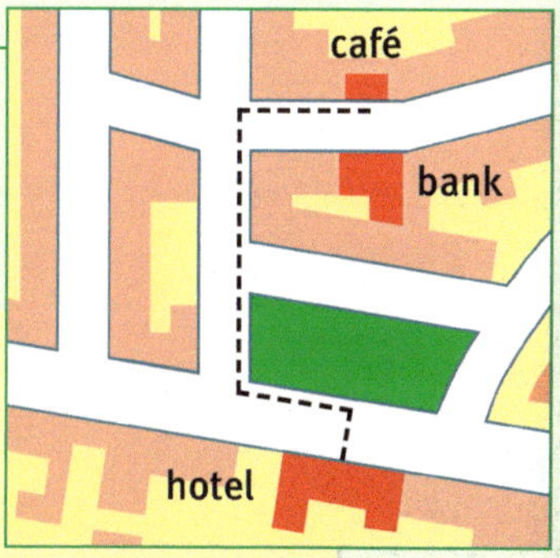

Sehen Sie sich den Stadtplan an. Ergänzen Sie dann die Wegbeschreibung von Ihrem Hotel zum Hot Box Café.

When you come out of the hotel, _ _ _ _ _ over the road and turn _ _ _ _. Take the _ _ _ _ _ street on the _ _ _ _ _ and go _ _ _ _ _ _ _ _ _ on. Take the _ _ _ _ _ _ street on the _ _ _ _ _ and the Hot Box Café is a little further along on your _ _ _ _, _ _ _ _ _ _ _ _ _ a bank.

6 Mix and match

Verbinden Sie die zusammengehörigen Satzteile.

1 Excuse me, could you tell	☐	a do the buses run?
2 How much	☐	b far is it to the market?
3 Excuse me, how	☐	c does it cost?
4 Could you tell me	☐	d the market close?
5 How often	☐	e me the time, please?
6 Do you know where	☐	f the way to the escalator, please?
7 Could you tell me how	☐	g the nearest bus stop is?
8 Excuse me, when does	☐	h to get to the market, please?

p. 85

TOURIST TIP

Remember to check what injections you need before you go abroad. Get an International Certificate of Vaccination[1] from your doctor or from your travel agent to keep a record. You needn't have any injections for Hong Kong but for many countries in Asia you must have injections or tablets against yellow fever and malaria about one month before you go.

1 Certificate of Vaccination: Impfpass

UNIT 10
LI YUEN MARKET

Market in Hong Kong

1 Starter

Find out where other members of the class spent their last holiday. Then ask them questions with *How much …? / How many …?*

Here are some ideas: *wine – drink / photos – take / postcards – send / churches – visit / people – meet / English – speak / mountains – climb / sun cream – use / luggage – take / money – spend / etc.*

Answer with *A lot / Quite a lot / Not much / Not many / None* and give a few details.

> **Remember:** Use *many* when you can count the items: How many bottles of wine did you drink? Use *much* when you can't count the item: How much wine did you drink?

2 35 Camera repairs

照相机

Sam: Excuse me, could you help me, please? It's this digital camera. I think it's damaged. It isn't mine, you see, it's my brother's, so I don't know whether it's broken or whether I've done something wrong. Anyway, it doesn't work …

Assistant: Can I have a look? What's the problem exactly?

S: Well, I think the battery is faulty. When I press the button to switch it on, nothing happens.

A: Hmm, yes, I see. But look, the battery is working. This symbol here shows you that the battery is okay.

S: So what do you think is wrong? I hope I haven't broken it.

A: I don't know. You'll have to leave it with us for a few days.

S: Oh, but I can't do that. We're only here for another four days. It's our first visit to Hong Kong and I really want to take some more pictures. Perhaps I should buy a digital camera myself. They're much cheaper in Hong Kong than in Europe. When we're back home, my brother can take this one back to the shop.

A: Well, sir, we have exactly the same model here …

S: And how much does it cost?

A: Just 2950 Hong Kong dollars.

S: Hmm. That sounds a good price. I know my brother paid more than that in London. And how many pictures can I store on this camera?

A: With this camera you can store about 120 pictures. Very good for holidays!

S: That's excellent! And at least I know how this camera works. Right, I've decided. I'll buy it. Can I pay by credit card?

A: Yes, of course.

S: Okay, here you are. But could you tell me where the nearest cash point is? I need to withdraw some Hong Kong dollars, too. My girlfriend has planned a visit to the markets – this could be a very expensive day!

S: Well, I think there's one just across the street. There are lots of banks there, so I'm sure you'll find one …

市场

3 What's wrong?

How does Sam explain that something is wrong with his camera? Fill in the gaps:

1 It's _ _ _ k _ _ .   2 It _ _ _ _ _ ' _ w _ _ _ .   3 It's _ _ _ _ _ y.   4 It's _ _ _ _ g _ _ .

4 Why don't you ...?

Now use one of the phrases in Activity 3 to explain that something is wrong with the things in the pictures below, e.g. *My discman doesn't work. What should I do?*

Maybe someone in the class can offer some advice: *Well, you'll have to listen to the radio instead!*

You should ... / You'll have to ... / Why don't you ...? / You could ...

5 36 Shopping for clothes

Katy has spent the afternoon at Li Yuen market. Listen to the dialogue between Katy and a stall-holder and fill in the missing words:

Katy wanted to buy a 1 .... but she had a problem – she didn't know what 2 .... she needed so the stall-holder said she could 3 .... it on. She liked the style but the colour didn't 4 .... her. And it didn't 5 .... her – it was a bit too small. The stall-holder gave her a larger one in a different colour. Katy loved it – and then she began to haggle about the 6 ....

6 What would you like?

When you buy clothes, you can say:
I'd like *a/some* ..... . Can I try *it/them* on, please?
You want to buy these items – what would you say? • sandals • a jacket • a coat • jeans • shorts • a bikini • a pullover • trousers • a t-shirt • a dress?

Remember: There's a glass of beer on the table. (singular) There's some beer in the glass. (uncountable). There are some tables in the bar. (plural)

Look at this shopping list. How would you ask for these items? Begin with: *I'd like ...*

1 kg apples
orange juice
bananas
1 litre fruit juice

Now make a shopping list of five food items you can buy at the supermarket. Give it to another student and he/she will ask for the items.

7 Money

Make a wordsearch. Write any words you associate with *money* in this grid. (You can use a dictionary to help you.) The words can be written horizontally or vertically. Fill in the empty squares with any other letters.

When you have finished, change books with a partner. Try to find the words your partner has written.

Now work with another pair of students. In turn, define the words on your list so that they can guess the words, e.g. *You can get money from this machine.*

C	A	S	H	P	O	I	N	T

8 Talk about it

In small groups, talk about things which you have bought on holiday – for yourself or presents for other people. Say where and why you bought them.

Now look at the Language Focus on page 50 of Pocket Tourist.

UNIT 10
LI YUEN MARKET

Bank of China, Hong Kong

SELFSTUDY

In Unit 10 haben Sie gelernt: • wie man um Rat fragt • und über Geld spricht • welche Redewendungen man beim Einkaufen benutzt und • wie man zählbare sowie unzählbare Hauptwörter benutzt. Üben Sie nun, was Sie gelernt haben.

1 Believe it or not

Ergänzen Sie folgende Präpositionen:
into / of (2) / at / in / down / to / about / with / through

When you see the futuristic buildings of Hong Kong, and read (1) .... Hong Kong's hectic financial world, you probably think what a modern society it is. But Hong Kong is a mixture (2) .... modern and traditional cultures. We can see this when we look at buildings in Hong Kong more closely. One (3) .... the most modern buildings is the splendid Bank of China – 72 floors of blue glass and steel – but look (4) .... the unusual angles of the walls and doors. Why was it built like this? Because bad spirits are not very clever and can only travel (5) .... straight lines so they can't get into this bank! Look at other buildings in Hong Kong and you'll see that the doors of nearly all the buildings are diagonal (6) .... the street – so the bad spirits can't enter. Even the splendid new, modern appartment block, Citic Tower, was built (7) .... a hole through it so that dragons can come (8) .... the mountain, go through the hole and (9) .... the sea! And the newly-built Regent Hotel has a glass front so the dragons can come down from the Blackhead mountains and go straight (10) .... the glass wall to bathe in the sea. (Glass is no problem for a dragon!)

2 37 Listen and repeat

Sprechen Sie die Sätze nach.

1 Excuse me, could you help me, please?
2 I think it's damaged.
3 It doesn't work.
4 You'll have to take it back to the shop.
5 How much does it cost?
6 I'll buy it. Can I pay by credit card?
7 Could you tell me where the nearest cash point is, please?
8 I'd like some trousers and a matching jacket.
9 Can I try them on, please?
10 Do you have a larger size?

LANGUAGE AND CULTURE

In many Western cultures, the number thirteen is an 'unlucky' number and lots of hotels don't have rooms or floors with the number thirteen. But in Hong Kong and China people think the number four is unlucky. Most of the buildings in Hong Kong don't have a fourth, fourteenth or twenty-fourth floor because in Cantonese the word 'four' sounds like 'death'.

3 How much? or How many?

Schreiben Sie folgende Wörter jeweils in die richtige Spalte: water / information / people / women / children / tourists / money / dollars / time / weeks / beer / food

Countable nouns	Uncountable nouns

Benutzt man diese Begriffe mit zählbaren (c=countable) oder unzählbaren (u=uncountable) Substantiven?

not much ( ), not many ( ),
there are ( ), there is ( )

Setzen Sie nun die Ausdrücke in die richtige Spalte.

4 C-words

Finden Sie zu jedem Wort in der linken Spalte die passende Beschreibung auf der rechten Seite.

1 cheque	☐	a the money returned to you by a shopkeeper, for example
2 change	☐	b the money used in a particular country
3 currency	☐	c a small sheet of paper on which you can write the amount you want to spend
4 credit card	☐	d not paper money – usually round discs of metal
5 cash	☐	e a way of buying something and paying later
6 coins	☐	f actual money – not credit – in the form of notes or coins

5 Have a haggle!

Vervollständigen Sie zunächst die Sätze und bringen Sie sie dann in die richtige Reihenfolge, so dass sich ein Gespräch ergibt.

- [1] Well, sir, if those don't f i t, how about this pair? These are a size bigger. They're beautiful shoes.
- [ ] Too expensive, you say? Okay, you can have them for HK$[1] 600.
- [ ] No, I'll pay HK$ 500. And that's my final _ _ _ _ _ – take it or leave it.
- [ ] For you, sir, just HK$ 650.
- [ ] Hmm, HK$ 650. I don't know. Brown doesn't really _ _ _ _ me and I don't have any brown trousers.
- [ ] Yes, they are nice. And how much do they _ _ _ _?
- [ ] No, thanks. I don't want any trousers, I just want _ _ _ _ new shoes. But they're much too expensive. I'll think about it.
- [ ] Sorry, sir. We only take _ _ _ _.
- [ ] No problem, sir. We have brown trousers, too. Very good quality!
- [ ] Right! 550 HK$.I'll take them. Can I pay _ _ credit card?
- [ ] What? 500 HK$? Just 50 HK$ more. You can have them for 550 HK$.

1 HK$: Hong Kong dollars

p. 86

Hong Kong street market

TOURIST TIP

You can often get a bargain[1] when you go shopping in markets abroad. But in many countries you shouldn't pay the first price they tell you – you have to haggle! So learn a few phrases to help you: *No, that's much too expensive. / I'll pay xxx and that's my final offer. / I'll think about it. / It's much cheaper in the shop.*

1 bargain: Gelegenheitskauf

UNIT 11
WISH YOU WERE HERE

1 Starter

Choose one of the words from the list below and act it out – without speaking – for the rest of the class to guess.

angrily / carefully / difficult / enormous / happy / heavy / old / politely / quietly / slowly

2 A postcard home

Hi Thomas,

How are things at the hospital? This holiday is amazing. We spent a fantastic fortnight in Australia. We climbed Sydney Harbour Bridge, flew over the Blue Mountains in a balloon and ate kangaroo! (Oh yes – I nearly forgot – the conference went very well, too!) Now we're in Hong Kong and it's wonderful. The hotel is a bit expensive but the staff are helpful and they speak English fluently – Cantonese is impossible! Tomorrow we're going to do a tour of the islands and we're going to see a Chinese ballet on Kowloon – a bit of culture. And we are not going shopping tomorrow! (That's Katy's new hobby.) The last three weeks have gone really fast. Time goes so quickly when you're on holiday. Hope you're all working hard!

See you soon. All the best,

Sam.

P.S. Katy sends her regards.

3 Describing words

Underline five *adjectives* on the postcard. They give you information about a person or a thing.
1) *This holiday is amazing.*

Now put a circle round five adverbs of manner (how adverbs) They give you information about a verb. 1) *The conference went well.*

Remember: Most adverbs of manner end in *-ly* (e.g. *quickly*) – *hard, fast* and *well* are exceptions.

4 Adverb or adjective

With a partner, complete this table.

Adjective	Adverb
fluent	fluently
	carefully
	fast
dangerous	
quick	
	well
slow	
hard	
	politely

5 A row of three

Your teacher will divide the class into two teams, A and B, and draw a 6x6 grid on the board. Now your teacher will ask a student from team A to make a sentence with a word from Activity 4. If the sentence is correct, that student can write A in one of the squares. Then your teacher will ask a student from team B to make a sentence with one of the words. If the sentence is correct, that student can write B in one of the squares. The winners are the team with a row of three As or Bs – horizontally, diagonally or vertically.

6 Sightseeing

Look at these Hong Kong attractions. With a partner, decide on two things to do on your first day in Hong Kong: *We could ... / Let's ... / Why don't we ...?*

1 Aberdeen fishing village

Sail across the harbour on a traditional Chinese boat and see the local fishermen at work. You can also visit a jewellery factory and buy hand-made jewellery.

2 Ocean Park tour

870,000 square metres of parkland with aquariums, dolphin shows and giant pandas. Go on the cable car ride and see the park from the sky. And there's even a 3-D cinema!

3 Dolphin watching cruise

You can see the world's pinkest dolphins in the waters round Lantau island. The cruise will sail past Hong Kong International Airport and Tsing Ma Bridge. A perfect trip for photographers.

4 Hong Kong panorama

Experience a 12-minute helicopter ride over Hong Kong and then have a Chinese lunch at the famous Jumbo Restaurant before shopping in Stanley Market.

5 Night cruise

Sail on a modern Chinese cruise boat with unlimited free drinks. Then visit the Revolving 66 Restaurant and enjoy the 360° panoramic view of Hong Kong.

Now tell the class what you're going to do. Listen and find out the most popular attraction.

Remember: It's better to simplify this phrase:
We're going to ~~go to~~ the city.

7 Write a postcard

On a piece of paper, complete this postcard and "send" it to another member of the class.

Dear ...,
This holiday is absolutely... . We arrived here in the ... town of ... on ... morning. The hotel is ... and the people are very ... and most of them can speak English ... . Tomorrow we're going to see ... and ... . to everyone in the English course.
All the ...,
...

When you get a postcard, read it and then tell the class

- who it is from
- where it is from
- one thing this person is going to do

8 38 At the post office

First match the British and American expressions.

GB	US
1 post	☐ package
2 letterbox	☐ area code
3 parcel	☐ mailbox
4 dialling code	☐ mail

Now listen to the dialogue. Are they speaking American or British English? How do you know?

Listen again and fill in the missing words:

1 I'd like to .... this .... to Australia.
2 How long will it take to .... there ?
3 How much is a .... for a card to Europe?
4 And I'd like a .... , please.
5 Could you tell me the .... for Sydney, please?

9 Talk about it

Find out which students in your class have planned their next holiday. Ask each of them questions about their plans – what they're going to see and do, where and how long they're going to stay, how they're going to travel, etc.

Now look at the Language Focus on page 51 of Pocket Tourist.

UNIT 11
WISH YOU WERE HERE

SELFSTUDY

In Unit 11 haben Sie gelernt wie man: • eine Postkarte schreibt • im Postamt etwas einkauft • mit Adverbien ausdrückt, auf welche Art und Weise man etwas macht und • mit *going to* über ein geplantes Vorhaben in der Zukunft spricht. Üben Sie nun, was Sie gelernt haben.

1 Happy Valley

The most popular entertainment for the local people in Hong Kong is horse racing. Betting on horse races is the only legal kind of gambling in Hong Kong. The two famous racecourses are in Happy Valley (Hong Kong Island) and Sha Tin (New Territories). You can see races on Wednesday evenings and Saturday afternoons from September to July – when the weather is pleasant and not too hot. The first race was in 1846. But this sport is even more popular in the 21st century and today you can see mobile phone betting and even online betting. At these races, people bet as much money in one evening there as they do in one year in Germany. The biggest race is in February, on the evening of the Chinese New Year. In one race, if you're lucky, it is possible to win over a million dollars! The Hong Kong Jockey Club organises the races to make sure that all the gambling is fair. The club pays an enormous gambling tax each year and this money finances many social projects – medical care, education, sports and cultural facilities – and last year they gave HK$ 1 billion to the Hong Kong Tourist Board.

Finden Sie Wörter im Text, die das Gegenteil ausdrücken:

1 least / .... 3 last / .... 5 tiny / ....
2 cold / .... 4 smallest /.............................. 6 few / ....

Benutzen sie nun die Vorsilben *il-*, *un-* (4x) und *im-*, um das Gegenteil der folgenden Wörter auszudrücken, z.B. *unhappy*

7 .... popular 9 .... pleasant 11 .... possible
8 .... legal 10 .... lucky 12 .... fair

2 39 Listen and repeat

Sprechen Sie die Sätze nach.

1 I'd like to send a parcel.
2 How long will it take to get there?
3 How much will it cost?
4 Could I have ten stamps for postcards, please?
5 Could you repeat that, please?
6 The staff are helpful.
7 They speak English fluently.
8 Katy sends her regards.
9 What are you going to do?
10 We're going to South Africa next month.

LANGUAGE AND CULTURE

Tourists who visit countries with non-European cultures should be extra sensitive to cultural differences. For example, in Hong Kong, when you give someone your business card, it's polite to do this with two hands. And think about dress codes, too. In some countries you must take off your shoes or cover your head before you go into a temple or church. And, of course, it's not always appropriate to wear shorts or for women to sunbathe topless on the beach.

3 What is it?

Ordnen Sie die Buchstaben in der richtigen Reihenfolge, damit sich Dinge ergeben, die Sie im Postamt finden.

1 mptsa ....
2 theoneelp adcr...
3 prcael ....
4 leettr..
5 otps obx..

Dear Pat, Weather is here – wish you were beautiful. Your loving husband, Ed.

4 A postcard

Katy schreibt eine Postkarte an ihre Eltern. Ergänzen Sie im Satz jeweils das Adjektiv in Klammern oder das dazugehörige Adverb.

Dear Mum and Dad,

Sam and I arrived in Hong Kong (safe) .... yesterday. The flight was (fine) .... and this time all our suitcases arrived (punctual) ....! The hotel is (great) .... and they have given us some (interesting) .... brochures about sightseeing in Hong Kong so we can plan what we want to do. Hong Kong is an (amazing) .... city. Tomorrow we're going to do a tour of the other islands. I can't believe how (fast) .... this holiday is going. See you soon.

Love,

Katy (and Sam)

5 Entertainment

Streichen Sie die falsche Erklärung durch.

1 A cruise is a journey by *boat / plane.*
2 A coach trip is a trip by *bus / train.*
3 If you book in advance, you buy the tickets *just / some time* before the performance.
4 A play is something you can watch at the *theatre / stadium.*
5 A matinée performance is in the *evening / afternoon.*
6 A special offer is *cheaper / more expensive* than the normal price.
7 You can see an exhibition in a *gallery / theatre.*
8 A box office is where you can buy *tickets / drinks.*

6 What are they going to do?

Was haben die Personen vor? Bilden Sie Sätze mit *going to.*

1 Katy is in a telephone box with Padma's phone number. She ....
2 Sam has a bottle of shampoo in his hand. He ....
3 Katy and Sam have just bought some postcards and stamps. They ....

p. 86

TOURIST TIP

At the moment, German tourists need only a valid passport to spend one month in Hong Kong – they don't have to get a visa. Austrian and Swiss tourists can stay in Hong Kong for three months without a visa, but all European tourists must have a visa to travel to mainland China. The situation could change, however, so make sure that you get up-to-date information about the passport and visa requirements of your host country – and do it well in advance.

UNIT 12
HAVE A NICE FLIGHT!

1 Starter

Choose a member of the class and describe what he/she is wearing and where he/she is sitting. The rest of the class has to guess who the person is.

Remember: Use the *present progressive* to describe what someone *is doing* at this moment.

2 40 Check-in

Listen to Katy and Sam checking-in at Hong Kong Airport. Write down any details you hear about their flight.

Katy: Look Sam, British Airways check-in. There it is. Over there, where that policeman is standing.
Sam: Phew, I thought we would never make it. That was close – only half an hour to go before take off. I'm really hot in this coat!
K: Well, at least we're here. That shuttle to the airport took much longer than last time, but at least nobody is queueing. What are you doing?
S: I'm looking for the tickets – I'm sure I put them in my coat pocket ...
Assistant: Good afternoon. Can I see your tickets and passports, please?
S: Yes, here they are.
A: Thank you. Have you any luggage to check in, Mr Grainger?
S: Yes. There's one large suitcase and these two smaller ones – and that shoulder bag.
A: And what about that bag you're holding, sir?
S: That's my briefcase. I'm taking it with me as hand luggage, if that's okay?
K: And I'm just carrying my handbag.
A: That's fine, thank you. Did you pack everything yourselves?
S and K: Yes, we did.
A: And you didn't leave your luggage unattended at any time?
S and K: No, we didn't.
A: Are you carrying any knives or scissors or sharp objects?
S and K: No, nothing.
A: Fine. You're booked right through to Edinburgh. Your flight is BA 028 to London Heathrow and the departure gate is 25.
S: Gate 25? How do we get there?
A: Boarding is on level 6. This is level 7, so you have to go down one floor. The lifts are over there – can you see where those children are sitting?
K: Oh, yes. Thanks. And is the flight on time?
A: I'm afraid your flight to London is a little delayed, so you can relax – they aren't boarding just yet. The plane should be ready for boarding at 17.45.
S: Oh, we have lots of time after all.
A: Here are your boarding cards.
S: Thanks very much.
A: You're welcome. Have a nice flight!
K: Yes, thank you. We've really enjoyed our stay. Goodbye!

3 40 Leaving Hong Kong

Listen to the dialogue again and answer the questions.

1 Where is the policeman standing?
2 What is Sam wearing?
3 How many people are waiting to check in?
4 How many pieces of luggage are Sam and Katy checking in?
5 What is Katy carrying?
6 Where are the children sitting?

4 What are they doing?

Write the *ing*-form of these verbs: check / speak / take / wait / show / stand / drink / eat / carry / write / sit / put / give.

> **Remember:** Verbs ending in *-e* usually lose the *-e* when you add *-ing: drive – driving*. And some verbs double the last letter: *swim – swimming.*

Now make a sentence about someone at an airport, using one of the above verbs in the present progressive, e.g. *The security guard is(n't) checking the luggage*. Then choose a verb and ask another student to make a sentence.

5 Spot the difference

Work with a partner. Student A, please look at page 77. Student B, please look at page 79.

6 First things first

Write numbers in the boxes to show in which order Katy and Sam did these things.

☐ They handed over their passports and tickets.
☐ They packed their suitcases and bags.
☐ They put a label on their luggage.
☐ They took the shuttle to the airport.
☐ They took the lift to level 6.
☐ They asked how to get to the departure gate.
☐ They found out where the check-in desk was.

7 Join them up

Look at the sentences in Activity 6 again. Work with a partner. Use these sentences to write a paragraph and use some of the words below as links, e.g. *First Katy and Sam packed their suitcases and bags ...*

first / next / then / later / after that / finally

Now compare your paragraph with another pair of students.

8 Saying the right thing

When someone goes on holiday you can say *Have a nice trip!*
In small groups, decide when or where might you use the following expressions:

1 Cheers!
2 Congratulations!
3 Hard luck!
4 Good luck!
5 You're welcome!
6 Excuse me!
7 Bless you!
8 Don't worry about it!

Work out a short dialogue with a partner and use one of the above expressions. Then act out your dialogue to another pair of students but leave out the expression. Can they guess which expression you left out?

9 41 Romance in the air

Listen to the dialogue and underline the appropriate answers to questions 1-4.

1 How does Katy feel about going home?
excited / sad to leave Hong Kong / travel sick
2 How does Sam feel about going home?
wants to be back in Edinburgh / happy to leave Hong Kong / understands how Katy feels
3 What has Sam bought for Katy?
something they can both use / something typical of Australia / something to remind Katy of her visit to Hong Kong
4 The present he has wrapped up for her is:
something light / something heavy / something electrical
5 Finally, what do you think Sam gave to Katy on the airplane?

10 Talk about it

As you learnt in the last unit, in Hong Kong, if you hand a local person your business card, you must do this with both hands. What differences in behaviour have you experienced in other countries? In small groups, talk about any cultural travel tips you have found particularly useful.

Now look at the Language Focus on page 52 of Pocket Tourist.

UNIT 12
HAVE A NICE FLIGHT!

SELFSTUDY

In Unit 12 haben Sie gelernt wie man: • im Alltag gebräuchliche Ausdrücke verwendet • sich bedankt und auf Dank antwortet • mit dem *present progressive* darüber spricht, was im Moment gerade passiert und • was man beim Check-in am Flughafen sagt. Üben Sie nun, was Sie gelernt haben.

Traditional Chinese bride and groom

1 Chinese wedding customs

Unterstreichen Sie das richtige Wort:

Chinese law says that when a woman (1) *gets / becomes* married, she must take her husband's surname – if they have the same surname, they are not allowed to marry. Normally, a woman does not remarry if her first (2) *husband / man* dies. There is also a law preventing government officers from marrying actresses!

On the morning of a wedding, the groom's friends send a gift of (3) *live / life* geese[1]. Geese are used as symbols of marriage because they (4) *hold / keep* the same partner for their whole life. At the wedding, the groom (5) *wears / carries* ceremonial clothes and the bride puts her (6) *hair / hairs* up in the traditional style of married women. After the wedding feast, relatives, friends and neighbours go to the bedroom of the young (7) *pair / couple* to play tricks on them.

1 geese: Gänse

2 42 Listen and repeat

Sprechen Sie die Sätze nach.

1 What are you doing?
2 I'm looking for the tickets.
3 Here they are.
4 Phew! That was close.
5 How do we get there?
6 There it is, over there.
7 Don't worry about it!
8 We've really enjoyed our stay.
9 Thanks very much.
10 You're welcome!

3 What to say

Welche Antwort passt in der jeweiligen Situation?

Hard luck / Pardon? / Congratulations / Cheers / Bless you

1 Someone sneezes. ....

2 You didn't hear what I said.

....

3 You're having a drink with friends.

....

4 Katy and Sam are getting married.

....

5 I've missed my flight. ....

4 Many thanks

Streichen Sie die falschen Wörter durch:

- Thank you *so / strongly / very / really* much.
- Thanks *a dozen / a million / a lot / a mile*.

Unterstreichen Sie mögliche Antworten auf *Thank you*.

It's all right. / Please. / You're welcome. / It's okay.

LANGUAGE AND CULTURE

In Exercise 1 you learned about some Chinese wedding customs. In many Western countries women often keep their maiden name (the surname they had before they got married) or join it to their husband's surname to form a 'double-barrelled name', e.g. Katy Moers-Grainger. Sometimes you will see the word *née* used to indicate the name a woman was born with – her maiden name, e.g Katy Grainger *née* Moers.

5 What are they doing?

Bilden Sie Fragen und Antworten nach folgendem Muster:

The man with a hat / eat / sleep

Is the man with a hat eating or sleeping? He isn't eating, he's sleeping.

1 The skier / read / telephone

....

.... ?

....

2 The two children / queue / play

....

.... ?

....

3 The two people / complain / drink

....

.... ?

....

4 The three people / sleep / queue

....

.... ?

....

5 The large woman / stand / sit

....

.... ?

....

6 The rich lady / drink / complain

....

.... ?

....

6 43 What's happening?

Was passiert hier gerade?

1 The plane ....

2 Katy ....

3 Sam ....

4 Katy and Sam ....

7 Checking in

Bringen Sie folgenden Dialog zwischen einem Passagier (P) und der Person am Check-in (A) in die richtige Reihenfolge.

☐ A: Did you pack the case yourself?

☐ P: Yes, here they are.

☐ P: Thank you. Goodbye.

☐ P: No, I didn't – and before you ask, I'm not carrying anything sharp or dangerous!

☐ P: Just the one suitcase – my laptop is hand luggage.

☐ A: Thank you. How many pieces of luggage are you checking in?

☐ A: I'm sorry, sir, but you know we must ask. Here's your boarding card. Your gate number is 16. Have a good flight.

☐ P: Yes, I did.

1 A: Good morning. Could I see your passport and ticket, please?

☐ A: And you didn't leave your case unattended at any time?

p. 86

TOURIST TIP

Nowadays checking in at the airport can take a long time, so it is best to confirm your check-in time before leaving for the airport. And most airlines are now very strict about what you can and cannot take with you onto a plane. Here are some of the objects one major airline forbids passengers to carry in their hand luggage:

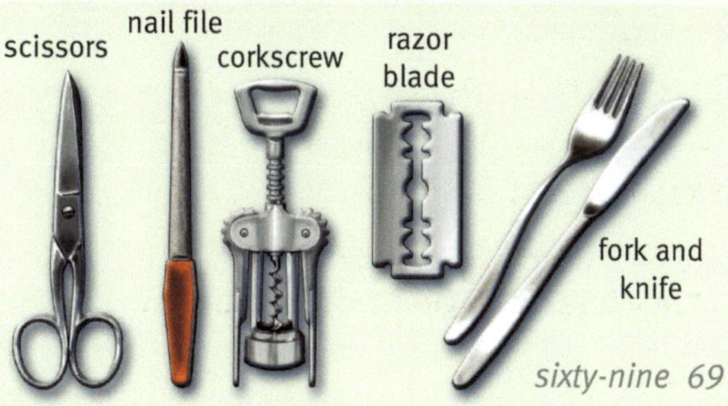

JAMAICAN HIGHLIGHTS
JAMAICAN HIGHLIGHTS

Have you ever been to the Caribbean? If you have, tell the class about some of your experiences.

JAMAICA, ISLAND IN THE SUN

There's a well-known song about Jamaica, *Island in the Sun*, by Harry Belafonte. And, with a year-round temperature of 29°C, it really *is* an island in the sun. Jamaica is the third largest island in the Caribbean and one million people live in its capital, Kingston. The first inhabitants of Jamaica were the Taino Indians and they called their island *Chaymaka* – well-watered – because it has over 100 rivers and lots of magnificent waterfalls. The Caribbean islands are also known as the West Indies because, when Columbus discovered them in 1492, he thought it was the west coast of India. The islands have very different characteristics and cultures, governments and languages. If someone from Barbados wants to fly to St Barthélemy, 650 kilometres away, he must get a visa, change planes twice, carry three different kinds of currency and show his passport four times!

Sunset in Negril

JAMAICAN RUM

When the Europeans – the Spanish, the French, the Dutch and the British – came to the Caribbean, they made money by producing sugar. They used the native islanders and African slaves to work on the sugar plantations. At first rum was just a waste product of the sugar and only these workers and slaves and the seamen drank it. But today, one of Jamaica's biggest exports is rum. The Latin name for sugar beet is *saccharum officinarum* and some people say that's how *rum* got its name!

JAMAICAN JERK

You can taste the influence of West Africa in West Indian cuisine[1]. The national dish is jerked pork or jerked chicken – very spicy grilled meat, usually barbecued and served with rice and beans ... and Red Stripe, Jamaican beer. Before your next barbecue, try mixing this Jamaican marinade and then cover some pieces of chicken with it for ten minutes before you grill them:

JAMAICAN CHICKEN WINGS

Mix a marinade of

- *3 pressed cloves[2] of garlic*
- *8 dessertspoons of oil*
- *6 dessertspoons of soya sauce*
- *2 dessertspoons of brown sugar*
- *juice of 1 lemon*
- *salt, pepper and cayenne pepper*

Did you know that the word *barbecue* got its name from the Taino Indians? They roasted iguanas and turtles on their *barbacoa* (grill).

- What meals are typical of the area where you come from?

[1]cuisine: Küche, Kochkunst

[2]clove: Zehe, Knolle

LANGUAGE CORNER

Like most things in the West Indies, the languages on the islands are a colourful mixture of influences. The Taino indians had their own language and then, in the fifteenth century, the Europeans and Africans arrived in the West Indies and influenced the language. On Jamaica the children learn English and Patois. Can you match these "Jamaica Talk" phrases with the standard English phrases?

1 Eye water	☐ a Everything OK
2 Cool runnings	☐ b Abroad
3 Up So	☐ c Tears
4 In foreign	☐ d Understood?
5 Seen?	☐ e Hello!
6 Yao!	☐ f USA

p. 86

JAMAICAN HIGHLIGHTS
SPOTLIGHT ON JAMAICAN PEOPLE

SIR HENRY MORGAN

(1635-88), pirate and governor

In the 1650s, Jamaica was an important harbour for the British pirates who attacked Spanish and French ships. The most famous pirate of them all was the Welshman Henry Morgan. He was such an enthusiastic pirate that, when Spain and England were at peace, Morgan continued to attack Spanish ships. He was put in prison in 1672 but, some years later, when Spain and England were fighting again, King Charles II made Morgan Governor of Jamaica.

REGGAE STAR BOB MARLEY

Bob Marley (1945-1981) is probably the most famous Jamaican. He made reggae music internationally famous with songs like *No woman, no cry* and *I shot the sheriff*. He died of cancer when he was 36 – but he was already a cult figure. When people hear the name Bob Marley, they think of reggae music and dreadlocks[1]!

Dreadlocks first became popular in Jamaica in the mid-1930s. People with this hairstyle called themselves Rastafarians after their Messiah, Ras Ta Fari (the Emperor Haile Selassie of Ethiopia). Rasta is a religion which developed in the Jamaican slums and it teaches that black West Indians will return to Africa.

1 dreadlocks: Rastalocken

WINSTON WATT

Winston Watt is one of Jamaica's leading sportsmen. A cricketer? No. An athlete? No. And not a basketball star. Winston is a member of Jamaica's Olympic *bobsleigh* team! Yes, Jamaica is one of the 28 countries which sends a bobsleigh team to the Olympic Games – although Jamaica's average winter temperature is 27°C. And how do they practise this winter sport when there is no snow? They have a bob with wheels on it – like a go-cart. At first it was difficult for their Norwegian trainer to explain to them what bobsleighing is – most of the team had never seen snow! In the 1990s, a film – *Cool Runnings* (Jamaica Talk for *Alles Okay*) – was made about these unusual Jamaican sportsmen who have even won medals in international events!

Dr No

IAN FLEMING

Creator of 007

Many famous people have spent a lot of time on Jamaica, including the actors Errol Flynn, Liz Taylor, Sean Connery, David Niven and Charlie Chaplin. Another famous person who made his home there was the author Ian Fleming, creator of 007. Fleming loved the climate and wildlife of Jamaica and that's where he wrote most of his James Bond books. When Fleming wrote the first 007 story, he couldn't think of a name for the character so he picked up one of his favourite books – *Birds of the West Indies* – and gave his character the name of the author. And so James Bond was born. Some of the Bond books were filmed on Jamaica: *Dr No* in the Blue Mountains and *Live and Let Die* in Montego Bay.

THE INHABITANTS OF SEAFORD TOWN

At first, the little village of Seaford Town in the highlands south-west of Cockpit Country looks just like any other Jamaican village. But when you meet the inhabitants of this village, you see that many of them have blond hair and blue eyes. Their great-grandparents were from Germany. In the early 1800s, there was very little work in Germany and a group of Germans went to Jamaica to try to be farmers. Their plans didn't work out well and even today the people in this village are very poor.

PUZZLE CORNER

Each two clues share a letter. Write the answers to the two clues in the squares.

- ↓ He discovered the West Indies.
- → The West Indies are in this sea.
- ↓ Jamaica's national food.
- → The capital of Jamaica.
- → Bob Marley's music.
- ↓ Jamaica's national drink.
- ↓ A Jamaican dialect.
- → The "German" village in Jamaica.
- ↓ The Indians who gave Jamaica its name.
- → Where *Live and Let Die* was filmed.

p. 86

The Adventures of Ivor Problem and Annie Mergency

AT THE HOTEL RECEPTION

Annie und Ivor erleben einige Überraschungen, als sie im Hotel ankommen.

Wenn Sie diese Geschichte lesen, aufschreiben oder nachspielen, können Sie die markierten Ausdrücke jeweils durch einen anderen Ausdruck in der gleichen Farbe ersetzen. Weitere nützliche Wörter und Redewendungen können Sie auf den entsprechenden Seiten in Pocket Tourist auf den Seiten 8-11 finden.

first, second

lunch, dinner

broken, faulty

speak to, complain to

must, need to

along the corridor, opposite the bar

damn, hell

Why don't you, I think you should

person in charge, your boss

the sauna, the cocktail bar

it's too small, it's not my size

brown shoes, yellow socks

Unit 2, activity 8, page 15

Memory Game

Partner A + B: Sehen Sie sich eine Minute lang den Stadtplan von Glenfellet an und versuchen Sie, sich an so viele Details wie möglich zu erinnern.

Bilden Sie nach folgendem Muster zwei Fragen über Glenfellet und schreiben Sie sie auf: *Is there a / an ...? Are there any ...?*

Benutzen Sie folgende Begriffe: *churches / airport / station / hotels / cathedral / museum / zoo / hospital / cinemas / art gallery / library / university / castle / parks / football stadium / town hall / golf course / theatres / sports centre.*

Partner B: Blättern Sie zurück auf Seite 15 und beantworten Sie die Fragen von Partner A mit den Formulierungen in Activity 8.

Partner A: Stellen Sie Ihre Fragen jemandem in Team B. Diese Person bekommt einen Punkt für jede richtige Antwort. Nachdem jeder in Team A eine Frage gestellt hat, stellen Mitglieder des Teams B ihre Frage.

Partner B: Stellen Sie nun Ihre Fragen an jemanden in Team A.

Unit 4, activity 9, page 23

Partner A: Sehen Sie sich die Informationen in den Kästchen an. Stellen Sie damit abwechselnd mit Ihrem Partner Fragen über die Zugverbindungen der einzelnen Städte. Antworten Sie jeweils auf die Fragen Ihres Partners. Notieren Sie jede Information, die Sie von Ihrem Partner bekommen und vergleichen Sie nach Abschluss der Übung Ihre Notizen mit denen Ihres Partners.

Example:

A: I'd like a return ticket to Edinburgh, please.
B: When would you like to travel?
A: On Thursday afternoon.
B: Well, there's a train at 2.20 p.m.
A: And what time does it arrive in Edinburgh?
B: At ten to four.
A: And do I have to change?
B: No, it's a direct train.

You start:	*Oban*	*You start:*
◁▷ to Wick	When?	▷ to Dunbar
Sat. morn	10.40 a.m.	Fri. eve
Arrival time?	12.52 p.m.	Arrival time?
Change?	Glasgow	Change?

Perth	*You start:*	*Stirling*
When?	◁▷ to Glasgow	When?
2.35 p.m.	Wed. p.m.	7.30 p.m.
3.20 p.m.	Arrival time?	9.52 p.m.
Direct	Change?	Edinburgh

(Note: ▷ is a single ticket; ◁▷ is a return ticket)

Unit 5, activity 10, page 33

Partner A: Sehen Sie sich diese Sätze aus einem Telefongespräch kurz an. Führen Sie nun ein kurzes Telefongespräch mit Ihrem Partner. Beginnen Sie. Ihr Partner wählt eine Antwort aus. Tauschen Sie die Rollen, wenn Sie zwei Telefongespräche geführt haben. Probieren Sie aus, wie viele verschiedene Gespräche Sie führen können.
Verwenden Sie eine Auswahl folgender Sätze:

Unit 8, activity 8, page 45

Partner A:

Part 1:
Hören Sie zu wie Katy und Sam über den Ort sprechen, die sie vom Heissluftballon aus sehen. Schreiben Sie folgende Begriffe an die richtigen Stellen in den Ortsplan: *filling station, post office, tourist information centre, golf course.*

Part 2:
Fragen Sie ein Mitglied der Gruppe B, wo sich folgende Einrichtungen befinden, damit Sie sie ebenfalls in Ihrem Ortsplan eintragen können: *caravan park, hotel, school*

Beantworten Sie dann die Fragen Ihres Partners. Dabei können Sie folgende Wörter benutzen: *next to, between, opposite, on the left, on the right, in front of, behind.*

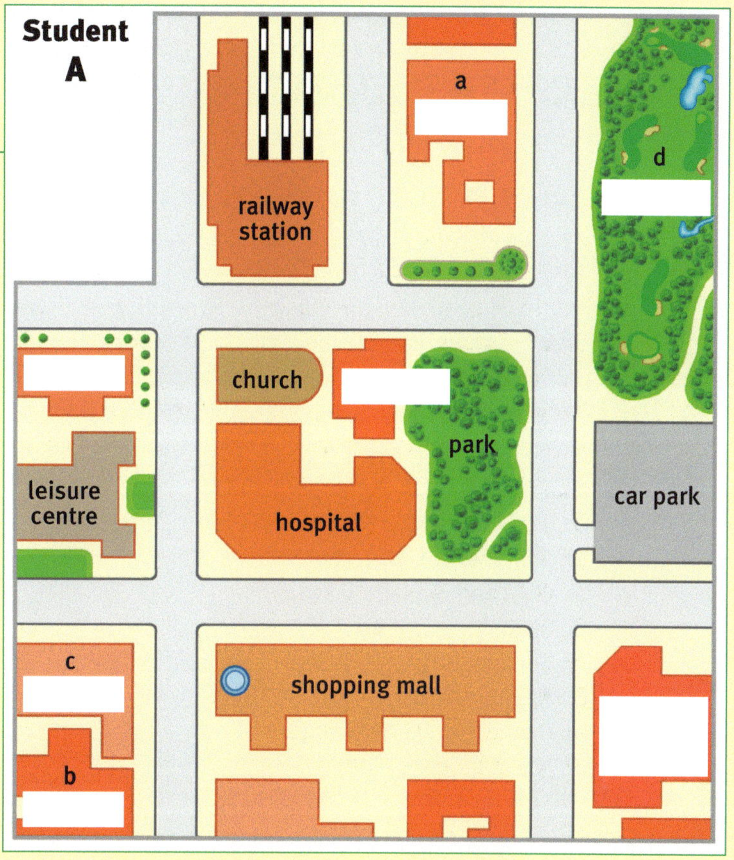

Unit 12, activity 5, page 67

Finden Sie die Unterschiede.

Partner A: Hier sehen Sie eine Warteschlange am Check-in eines Flughafens. Partner B hat ein fast gleich aussehendes Bild vor sich. Aber es gibt 10 kleine Unterschiede zwischen Bild A und Bild B. Stellen Sie sich gegenseitig abwechselnd Fragen, um diese Unterschiede herauszufinden, z.B. *What is the old man doing in your picture? What's he wearing? Where is he standing? Is he carrying anything? Is he smoking?* Notieren Sie alle Unterschiede, die Sie finden. Sehen Sie dazu nicht auf das Bild von Partner B.

Berichten Sie nach 5 Minuten alle Unterschiede, die Sie bis dahin gefunden haben, Ihrer Lerngruppe: *In picture A the old man isn't smoking; in picture B, he is. etc.*

Unit 4, activity 9, page 23

Partner B: Sehen Sie sich die Informationen in den Kästchen an. Stellen Sie damit abwechselnd mit Ihrem Partner Fragen über die Zugverbindungen der einzelnen Städte. Antworten Sie jeweils auf die Fragen Ihres Partners. Notieren Sie jede Information, die Sie von Ihrem Partner bekommen und vergleichen Sie nach Abschluss der Übung Ihre Notizen mit denen Ihres Partners.

Example:

A: I'd like a return ticket to Edinburgh, please.
B: When would you like to travel?
A: On Thursday afternoon.
B: Well, there's a train at 2.20 p.m.
A: And what time does it arrive in Edinburgh?
B: At ten to four.
A: And do I have to change?
B: No, it's a direct train.

Wick	**You start:**	**Dunbar**
When? 8.40 a.m. 12.55 p.m. Inverness	◁▷ to Oban Tues. a.m. Arrival time? Change?	When? 7.25 p.m. 9.20 p.m. Edinburgh
You start: ◁▷ to Perth Sun. p.m. Arrival time? Change?	**Glasgow** When? 2.35 p.m. 3.20 p.m. Direct	**You start:** ▷ to Stirling Mon. eve Arrival time? Change?

(Note: ▷ is a single ticket; ◁▷ is a return ticket)

Unit 5, activity 10, page 33

Partner B: Sehen Sie sich diese Sätze aus einem Telefongespräch kurz an. Führen Sie nun ein kurzes Telefongespräch mit Ihrem Partner. Ihr Partner beginnt. Wählen Sie eine Antwort aus. Tauschen Sie die Rollen, wenn Sie zwei Telefongespräche geführt haben. Probieren Sie aus, wie viele verschiedene Gespräche Sie führen können.
Verwenden Sie eine Auswahl folgender Sätze:

Yes, the code is 0191 for Newcastle, then it's 2399856.

Hi, it's Alex here. Can I speak to Frank, please?

Thanks. Can you ask him to call me when he gets in?

Thanks very much.

Thanks. Could you ask him to ring me back?

No, it's all right. I'll ring back later. Do you know when he'll be back?

Oh right. I'll try his mobile. Do you have his number?

Could you say that again, plea-se?

Alex Davies. D – A – V – I – E – S.

Oh, I'm terribly sorry.

Goodbye.

Unit 8, activity 8, page 45

Partner B:

Part 1:
Hören Sie zu wie Katy und Sam über den Ort sprechen, die sie vom Heissluftballon aus sehen. Schreiben Sie folgende Begriffe an die richtigen Stellen in den Ortsplan: *filling station, post office, tourist information centre, golf course.*

Part 2:
Suchen Sie sich nun einen Partner aus Gruppe A und beantworten Sie seine Fragen. Dabei können Sie folgende Wörter benutzen: *next to, between, opposite, on the left, on the right, in front of, behind.*

Fragen Sie nun Ihren Partner, wo sich folgende Einrichtungen befinden, damit Sie sie ebenfalls in Ihrem Ortsplan eintragen können: *park, leisure centre, hospital.*

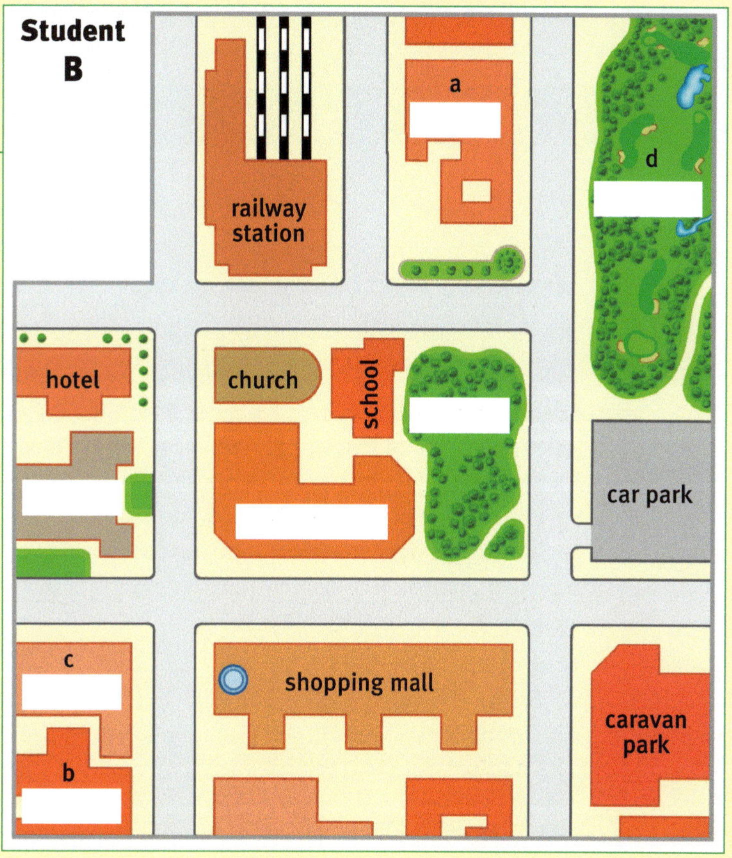

Unit 12, activity 5, page 67

Finden Sie die Unterschiede.

Partner B: Hier sehen Sie eine eine Warteschlange am Check-in eines Flughafens. Partner A hat ein fast gleich aussehendes Bild vor sich. Aber es gibt 10 kleine Unterschiede zwischen Bild A und Bild B. Stellen Sie sich gegenseitig abwechselnd Fragen, um diese Unterschiede herauszufinden, z.B. *What is the old man doing in your picture? What's he wearing? Where is he standing? Is he carrying anything? Is he smoking?* Notieren Sie alle Unterschiede, die Sie finden. Sehen Sie dazu nicht auf das Bild von Partner A.

Berichten Sie nach 5 Minuten alle Unterschiede, die Sie bis dahin gefunden haben, Ihrer Lerngruppe:
In picture A the old man isn't smoking; in picture B, he is. etc.

GAMES

Unit 6, activity 8, page 37

The restaurant game: A game for groups of three or pairs.

Jeder Spieler braucht eine kleine Münze als Spielfigur; zusätzlich ist eine große Münze nötig.

Überlegen Sie sich, welche Rolle Sie übernehmen wollen. Legen Sie eine der kleinen Münzen auf das Spielfeld, das Ihre Figur zeigt. Wenn Sie an der Reihe sind, werfen Sie die große Münze: Kopf: ziehen Sie ein Spielfeld nach vorne; Zahl: ziehen Sie zwei Felder nach vorne. Machen Sie, was auf dem jeweiligen Spielfeld verlangt ist. Auf den Feldern mit den Illustrationen brauchen Sie nichts zu tun. *Miss a turn* bedeutet: Sie müssen eine Runde aussetzen. Wer zuerst Nummer 12 erreicht hat, hat gewonnen.

Unit 5, activity 4, page 33

Suitcase Bingo

Wenn Sie jetzt für 2 Wochen wegfahren könnten, welchen Urlaub würden Sie machen? Eine Safari in Afrika, einen Skiurlaub in Kanada, eine Kulturreise in Großbritannien, einen Strandurlaub in Jamaica, einen Campingurlaub in Irland oder eine Kreuzfahrt auf dem Atlantik. Was packen Sie in Ihren Koffer?

Tragen Sie in jedes Kästchen des Koffers einen Gegenstand ein, den Sie mitnehmen. Ihr/e Kursleiter/in wird nun verschiedene Gegenstände nennen. Wenn sich die genannten Gegenstände in Ihrem Koffer befinden, streichen Sie sie durch.

Wer zuerst 3 Kreuze in einer waagrechten, senkrechten oder diagonalen Reihe hat, hat gewonnen. Der Gewinner liest laut vor, was in seinem Koffer ist. Der Kurs soll erraten, für welche Art Urlaub der Gewinner sich entschieden hat.

Unit 9, activity 9, page 55

Chinese Chequers

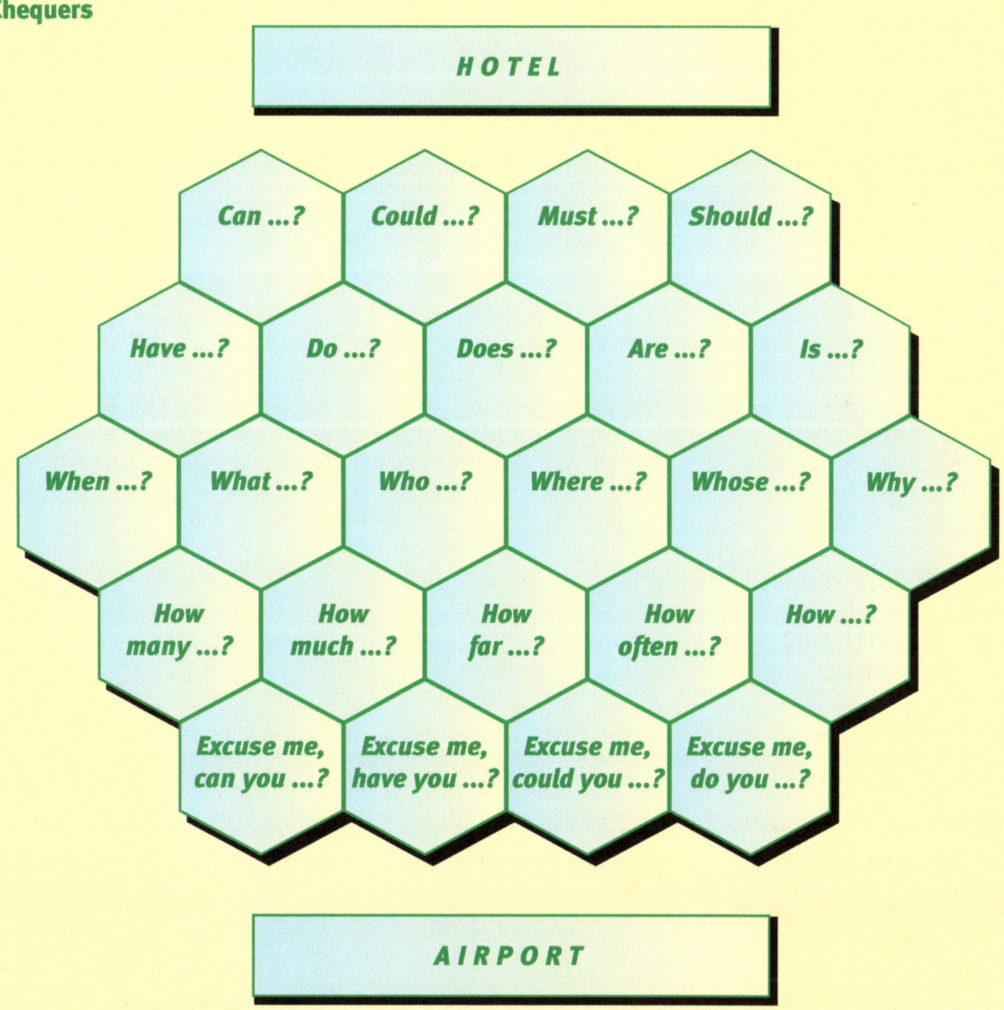

Bilden Sie Zweier-, Dreier- oder Vierergruppen. Sie gehen vom Flughafen zum Hotel. Bewegen Sie sich abwechselnd ein Feld in eine beliebige Richtung und bilden Sie jeweils eine Frage mit den im Zielfeld angegebenen Worten. Es kann nur ein Spieler auf einem Feld sein. Fangen Sie das Spiel an, indem Sie eine Münze auf das Feld mit den Worten *Excuse me* setzen.

INTERNET PROJECT
HOROSCOPES

The Chinese Zodiac

Katy und Sam waren in Hong Kong bei einer Wahrsagerin und haben sich ihre gemeinsame Zukunft voraussagen lassen. Zuerst mussten sie ihr Geburtsjahr angeben, woraufhin ihnen die Wahrsagerin ihr chinesisches Horoskop-Zeichen nannte. Das chinesische Horoskop basiert auf einem 12-Jahres-Zyklus, bei dem jedes Jahr durch ein anderes Tier mit bestimmten Charakteristika repräsentiert wird.

Katy was born in 1979 – the year of the Goat, and Sam was born in 1975 – the year of the Rabbit. Look at the Goat and the Rabbit and write down what Katy's and Sam's characteristics are. If there's a word you don't understand, look at the word list on page 87.

鷄 **Rooster** (Hahn)
patriotic
aggressive
hard-working

猴 **Monkey** (Affe)
humorous
restless
imaginative

猪 **Pig** (Schwein)
generous
materialistic
naive

犬 **Dog** (Hund)
pessimistic
honest
introverted

羊 **Goat** (Ziege)
artistic
dependent
kind

兔 **Rabbit** (Hase)
snobbish
thoughtful
wise

鼠 **Rat** (Ratte)
charismatic
intelligent
greedy

馬 **Horse** (Pferd)
friendly
impatient
witty

蛇 **Snake** (Schlange)
discreet
possessive
manipulative

龍 **Dragon** (Drache)
arrogant
enthusiastic
original

虎 **Tiger** (Tiger)
energetic
optimistic
impulsive

牛 **Ox** (Ochse)
popular
inflexible
loyal

Work with a partner. Read the characteristics of the different signs. Which sign do you think you are? Now find out if you were right! What was the year of your birth? Which sign are you? (If your birth year isn't on the list, you can work it out by writing another line of years.)

Dog	Pig	Rat	Ox	Tiger	Rabbit	Dragon	Snake	Horse	Goat	Monkey	Rooster
1946	1947	1948	1949	1950	1951	1952	1953	1954	1955	1956	1957
1958	1959	1960	1961	1962	1963	1964	1965	1966	1967	1968	1969
1970	1971	1972	1973	1974	1975	1976	1977	1978	1979	1980	1981
1982	1983	1984	1985	1986	1987	1988	1989	1990	1991	1992	1993

Which three characteristics are typical of your sign? Is this true of you?

Do you think anyone in your class is similar in character to you? Ask them what his/her sign is and find out if you both have the same one.

WWW. Gehen Sie zu www.englishnetworklink.com/horoscope und wählen Sie ein Tierzeichen. Passen Katy (goat) und Sam (rabbit) zusammen?

SCHLÜSSEL
SELFSTUDY

Unit 1

Unit 1, exercise 1
1 is 2 has 3 call 4 doesn't have 5 is 6 ski 7 snows 8 snows 9 rains 10 know 11 don't wear 12 don't play 13 does ... eat 14 drinks 15 Do ... know

Unit 1, exercise 3
1e, 2c, 3f, 4a, 5d, 6b

Unit 1, exercise 4
1 ~~Do~~ 2 ~~a~~ 3 ~~How~~ 4 ~~Does~~ 5 ~~Is~~ 6 ~~has~~ 7 ~~drives~~ 8 ~~does~~ 9 ~~fly~~

Unit 1, exercise 5
1 What's his name? 2 Where does he live? 3 Where does he come from? / Where is he from? 4 What does he do? / What's is job?

Unit 1, exercise 6
1 Liz is English. 2 She lives in Stuttgart. 3 She's married. 4 She has one daughter and a son. / She's got one daughter and a son. 5 She doesn't always work in Stuttgart. 6 She really likes her job. 7 She speaks French. 8 She's looking forward to going to Italy.

Unit 1, exercise 7
1 Yes, she can. 2 No, she isn't. Yes, she does. 4 Yes, she is. 5 No, they aren't. 6 Yes, they do. 7 No, they don't.

Unit 2

Unit 2, exercise 1
1 lots of 2 some 3 an 4 some 5 any 6 a

Unit 2, exercise 3
1 ~~in the~~ 2 ~~to~~ 3 ~~twelve~~ 4 ~~on~~

Unit 2, exercise 4
1 half past nine in the morning 2 quarter past three in the afternoon 3 twenty-five to nine in the evening 4 five past eleven at night 5 twelve o'clock, midday

Unit 2, exercise 5
A: is, a B: are, an A: is, a B: there, some A: are, any B: an

Unit 2, exercise 6
1 Let's ... 2 We could ... 3 Why don't we ...

Unit 2, exercise 7
1 in December 2 at 12 o'clock, midnight 3 in winter and in summer 4 at the weekend 5 on Sundays

Unit 3

Unit 3, exercise 1
1 famous 2 most famous 3 oldest 4 small 5 bigger 6 best 7 most surprising

Unit 3, exercise 3
1b, 2a, 3d, 4e, 5c

Unit 3, exercise 4
1 was 2 were 3 were 4 wasn't 5 was 6 were 7 weren't 8 were 9 were 10 was

Unit 3, exercise 5
1 big 2 friendly 3 interesting 4 good 5 bad
1 big, bigger, biggest 2 friendly, friendlier, friendliest 3 interesting, more interesting, the most interesting 4 good, better, the best 5 bad, worse, the worst

Unit 3, exercise 6
1 Where were you in summer?
2 Was your hotel very expensive?
3 Was the weather worse than here?
4 What were the people like?
5 What would you like to drink?
6 Could you bring me a gin and tonic, please?
7 Could I have a pint of beer, please?
8 Would you like a lager?

Unit 4

Unit 4, exercise 1

1 did ... ask 2 started 3 didn't want 4 ran 5 was 6 went 7 met 8 fell 9 told 10 wanted 11 said 12 rode 13 got 14 followed 15 tried 16 didn't find 17 left 18 went

Unit 4, exercise 3

1 themselves 2 ourselves 3 himself 4 yourself 5 herself

Unit 4, exercise 4

2 ...has to explain it. 3 ...has to drive. 4 ...don't have to book. 5 ...don't have to pay.

Unit 4, exercise 5

1 tickets 2 after 3 forward 4 have 5 nice 6 Enjoy 7 postcard 8 four

Unit 4, exercise 6

1f, 2e, 3a, 4g, 5d, 6b, 7c

Language and culture:

An American would put his/her baggage into a cab; A British person would put his/her luggage into a taxi.

Highlight 1

Puzzle Corner

George Washington, Thomas Jefferson, Theodore Roosevelt, Abraham Lincoln

Language Corner

1d, 2g, 3k, 4a, 5l, 6h, 7b, 8i, 9c, 10f, 11e, 12j

Unit 5

Unit 5, exercise 1

1 F 2 T 3 F 4 T 5 T 6 F

Unit 5, exercise 3

1c, 2d, 3b, 4a

Unit 5, exercise 4

black trousers, green jacket, beige suit, yellow blouse, red dress, brown pullover, white shirt

Unit 5, exercise 5

You ... your, He ... his, her ... hers, We ... ours, They ... theirs

Unit 5, exercise 6

1 Liz is Rolf's wife. 2 Barbara is Ben's sister. 3 Rolf is Robin's father. 4 Barbara is Liz's grand-daughter. 5 Katy is Ben's aunt. 6 Ben is Katy's nephew.

Unit 5, exercise 7

1 Hello, this is Katy. 2 Could I speak to Dad, please? 3 Hold on a moment, please. 4 What's the dialling code for Austria, please?

Unit 5, exercise 8

1 Paul is my friend's son. 2 I packed blue jeans and a green pullover. 3 Whose is this camera? It isn't mine. 4 Excuse me, waiter – could we have the bill, please? 5 Hello, this is Pam. 6 Where is my key – can you see it?

Unit 6

Unit 6, exercise 1

1 temperatures 2 rain 3 storms 4 winds 5 weather 6 tropical 7 milder 8 snows 9 seasons 10 summer 11 sunshine

Unit 6, exercise 3

1 ~~order~~ 2 ~~glass wine~~ 3 ~~Hello~~ 4 ~~I like~~ 5 ~~I have~~ 6 ~~pay~~

Unit 6, exercise 4

2 I'm sorry but this knife is dirty. 3 I'm sorry but this tea's cold. 4 I'm sorry but these rolls aren't fresh. 5 I'm sorry but this bill is wrong.

Unit 6, exercise 5

1b 2d 3a 4c

Unit 6, exercise 6

2 ... they'll go to Paris / France. 3 ... they'll go to Moscow / Russia. 4 They'll go to New York / America.

Unit 7

Unit 7, exercise 1

1 13,000 thirteen thousand
2 30 thirty
3 19.000.000 nineteen million
4 40% forty percent
5 120° one hundred and twenty degrees
6 250 two hundred and fifty

Unit 7, exercise 3

1 Sam has climbed the Statue of Liberty. 2 Katy has never done anything like that. 3 She has taken lots of photos. 4 Have you ever eaten Japanese food? 5 I haven't met Katy's mother.

Unit 7, exercise 4

1 Have they ever drunk Australian beer? 2 Did you give the waiter a tip after dinner? 3 What time did the plane take off? 4 Has he ever eaten ostrich? 5 Have you ever spoken to an American? 6 Did you swim in the sea last year?

Unit 7, exercise 5

1 **Have** you ever **seen** a crocodile? 2 No **I've (have)** never **seen** a crocodile but I**'ve (have) seen** an alligator. I **saw** one when I **went** to South Africa in 1999 3 I**'ve (have)** never **flown** in a helicopter. **Have** you ever **done** that? 4 My brother**'s (has) flown** in a helicopter. And he**'s (has) flown** in a sports plane, too. He **flew** over the Grand Canyon in America last year.

Unit 7, exercise 6

1 always speaks 2 rarely speaks 3 never speaks
4 usually speak 5 always speak

Unit 8

Unit 8, exercise 1

1 Have ... heard 2 haven't heard 3 have seen
4 has become 5 have built 6 have developed
7 have tried 8 have been 9 have died
10 have had

Unit 8, exercise 3

1 Surname 2 First name 3 Sex 4 Date of birth
5 Place of birth 6 Nationality 7 Occupation
8 Address 9 Phone number 10 Signature

Unit 8, exercise 4

1 Ningaloo 2 Cloncurry 3 Hughenden
4 Woolloomoolloo

Unit 8, exercise 5

1 should ... police station ... opposite 2 don't ... bakery ... between 3 should ... dental surgery ... above 4 Why ... post office ... right

Language and culture:

JB 007 is James Bond's car. E1 TON is Elton John's number plate. B G8S stands for Bill Gates. P1 LOT – the owner is a pilot. MPH 200 – this car can go very fast ... at 200 miles per hour. WE R4 = We are (a family of) four.

Highlight 2

Language Corner

1d, 2g, 3h, 4a, 5f, 6e, 7c, 8b

Puzzle Corner

1a, 2c, 3c, 4b, 5b

Unit 9

Unit 9, exercise 1

1 Ocean Park 2 Star Ferry 3 Feng-Shui Tour 4 Big Buddha 5 Victoria peak

Unit 9, exercise 3

1b, 2h, 3d, 4a, 5g, 6e, 7c, 8f

Unit 9, exercise 4

Family Name: Macpherson Mr ☑
Single room [2]
Double room [1]
Number of nights: 3
From: September 29th To: October 1st
Special requirements: An early breakfast on Monday
Credit card number: 4929 4044 5790 6001

Unit 9, exercise 5

cross, left, first, right, straight, second, right, left, opposite

Unit 9, exercise 6

1e, 2c, 3b, 4f, 5a, 6g, 7h, 8d

Unit 10

Unit 10, exercise 1

1 about 2 of 3 of 4 at 5 in 6 to 7 with 8 down 9 into 10 through

Unit 10, exercise 3

Countable nouns: people, women, children, tourists, dollars, weeks
Uncountable nouns: water, information, money, time, beer, food
not much (u), not many (c), there are (c), there is (u)

Unit 10, exercise 4

1c 2a 3b 4e 5f 6d

Unit 10, exercise 5

1 Could 2 Excuse 3 tell 4 should

Unit 10, exercise 6

1 fit, 7, 8 offer, 3, 4 suit, 2 cost, 6 some 11 cash, 5, 10 by, 9

Unit 11

Unit 11, exercise 1

1 most 2 hot 3 first 4 biggest 5 enormous 6 many 7 unpopular 8 illegal 9 unpleasant 10 unlucky 11 impossible 12 unfair

Unit 11, exercise 3

1 stamp 2 telephone card 3 parcel 4 letter 5 post box

Unit 11, exercise 4

safely fine punctually great interesting amazing fast

Unit 11, exercise 5

1 ~~plane~~ 2 ~~train~~ 3 ~~just~~ 4 ~~stadium~~ 5 ~~evening~~ 6 ~~more expensive~~ 7 ~~theatre~~ 8 ~~drinks~~

Unit 11, exercise 6

1 She's going to phone / call / telephone Padma. 2 He's going to wash his hair. 3 They're going to write some postcards.

Unit 12

Unit 12, exercise 1

1 gets 2 husband 3 live 4 keep 5 wears 6 hair 7 couple

Unit 12, exercise 3

1 Bless you 2 Pardon? 3 Cheers 4 Congratulations 5 Hard luck

Unit 12, exercise 4

Thank you so / ~~strongly~~ / very / ~~really~~ much.
Thanks ~~a dozen~~ / a million / a lot / ~~a mile~~.
It's all right. / You're welcome. / It's okay.

Unit 12, exercise 5

1 Is the skier reading or telephoning? She isn't reading, she's telephoning. 2 Are the two children queueing or playing? They aren't queueing, they're playing. 3 Are the two people drinking or complaining? They aren't drinking, they're complaining. 4 Are the three people sleeping or queueing? They aren't sleeping, they're queueing. 5 Is the large woman standing or sitting? She isn't standing, she's sitting.
6 Is the rich lady drinking or complaining? She isn't complaining, she's drinking.

Unit 12, exercise 6

1 ... is landing. 2 ... is reading a newspaper. 3 ... is having a shower. 4 ... are getting married.

Unit 12, exercise 7

5, 2, 10, 8, 4, 3, 9, 6, 1, 7

Highlight 3

Language Corner

1c, 2a, 3f, 4b, 5d, 6e

Puzzle Corner

COLUMBUS, CARIBBEAN, JERK, KINGSTON, REGGAE, RUM, PATOIS, SEAFORD, TAINO, MONTEGO

TAPESCRIPTS
SELFSTUDY

Unit 2, exercise 7

Tourist info: Good morning. Can I help you?
Male tourist: Yes, can you tell me if the castle is also open to visitors in December?
Tourist info: Yes, of course. But the hours are different – it closes a little earlier in December.

* * *

Female tourist: Hi, can you tell me what time the Hard Rock Café in George Street closes, please?
Tourist info: Sure, let me check ... Here we are, it's open from twelve o'clock midday to twelve o'clock midnight, seven days a week.
Female tourist: Great, thanks a lot. And what about the Ski Centre – is that open in the summer, too?
Tourist info: Yes, of course. It's open all year – in winter and in summer.

* * *

Male tourist: Good morning. We're in Edinburgh for the weekend and we'd like to play golf tomorrow. Are there any golf clubs near the city centre?
Tourist info: There are lots of clubs in the city, sir. For example ... look at this map ... there's one here at Braid Hills. That's also open to visitors at the weekend ...
Male tourist: Fine, that's perfect. And we want to visit the National Gallery of Scotland in the morning. Can you tell us what time it opens?
Tourist info: Ah, I'm sorry. The National Gallery of Scotland is closed on Sunday morning but it's open in the afternoon. It opens at midday on Sundays.

Unit 7, exercise 6

P: ... Yes, Klaus is having a few problems at the conference because of his English. You're lucky – you were brought up bi-lingually, weren't you?
K: Yes, that's right. When we were children, my mother spoke to my brother and me in English and my father spoke German to us. And even now my mother always speaks English to me.
P: What about your father? How good is his English?
K: Well, he can understand everything but he rarely speaks English at home – only when we have English visitors, of course. And at work – well, he never speaks English at work. When we go on holiday to England, he practises and he's not bad. But what about you? Your English is excellent.
P: Actually I was brought up bi-lingually, too.
K: Really? But isn't Hindi the language in India?
P: Yes, that's the *official* language – but there are nearly 900 other languages and dialects in India, too, so the one language people can communicate in is – English.
K: I see – so a lot of people speak both English and Hindi?
P: Yes, there are about a billion people in India so there are more English-speakers in India than in England!

INTERNET PROJECT
Vocabulary

aggressive	aggressiv	honest humo-	ehrlich	naive	naiv
arrogant	arrogant	rous	humorvoll	optimistic origi-	optimistisch
artistic	künstlerisch	imaginative	phantasievoll	nal	originell
charismatic	charismatisch	impatient	ungeduldig	patriotic	patriotisch
dependent	abhängig	impulsive	impulsiv	pessimistic	pessimistisch
discreet	diskret	inflexible intel-	unflexibel	popular	beliebt
energetic	energisch	ligent	intelligent	possessive	besitzgierig
enthusiastic	enthusiastisch	introverted	introvertiert	restless	unruhig
friendly	freundlich	kind	liebenswürdig	snobbish	vornehmtuend
generous	großzügig	loyal	loyal	thoughtful	rücksichtsvoll
greedy	gierig	manipulative	manipulierend	wise	weise
hard-working	fleißig	materialistic	materialistisch	witty	witzig

K: Really? And which language do you speak at home?

P: Well, we usually speak Hindi at home when the family's together but when we have guests then we always speak English.

K: Yes – that's like when we have guests and we all speak English ...

Unit 8, exercise 4

1 Ningaloo is a paradise for swimmers. It has a wonderful coral reef. Ningaloo? I'll spell it: N-I-N-G-A-L-double O.

2 Do you know what Cloncurry is famous for? It's the home of the Flying Doctor service. Cloncurry – that's C-L-O-N-C-U-double R-Y.

3 Last year I visited Hughenden. How do you spell it? H-U-G-H-E-N-D-E-N.

4 My cousin lives in Woolloomoolloo – great name, it's got nearly double everything! Listen, I'll spell it for you: W-double O-double L-double O-M-double O-double L-double O.

Unit 9, exercise 4

R: Imperial Hotel. Good morning. Can I help you?

C: Good morning. I'd like to make a room reservation for this weekend, please. Have you got any vacancies?

R: Yes, no problem sir. Can I just take your name, please?

C: Yes, it's Roderick Macpherson. I'll spell that for you: M-A-C-P-H-E-R-S-O-N.

R: And what sort of accommodation would you like exactly?

C: Well, there are four of us altogether. Ideally we would like a double room and two singles. But two doubles with twin beds would be okay.

R: No, that's fine sir. We have a double and two singles for this weekend. And for how many nights?

C: Three altogether. We arrive on Friday evening and we have to leave quite early on Monday morning.

R: OK, 29th, 30th September and 1st October. I've booked that for you. Is there anything else I can help you with before I take your credit card details?

C: Well, just one question. We have to be at the airport at 8 o'clock on Monday morning. That'll probably be too early for breakfast?

R: Well, yes. We normally serve breakfast from 7.30 till 10.30 at weekends. But I'm sure it will be possible to organise something – a pot of tea or coffee and some toast, at least. I'll make a note of it ...

C: That's very kind of you. Thanks very much for your help.

R: You're welcome. Now, if I can just take your credit card details, sir?

C: Oh, yes, sure. I have a Visa card with the number 4929 4044 5790 6001.

R: Could you repeat that number, please?

C: Yes, of course. 4929 4044 5790 6001.

R: And the expiry date, please?

C: Yes, just a minute. The expiry date is May ...

Unit 11, exercise 6

1 *K:* Sam, where's the shampoo? Have you seen it?
S: The shampoo? Yes – it's in the case – I haven't unpacked it. Do you need it?
K: Yes – can you bring it in, please?
S: Okay.

2 *K:* I know you don't like doing it but your parents will be disappointed if they don't get a card. You wrote one to Thomas.
S: Oh, all right, then. Have you got any stamps?
K: Yes, here they are.
S: And a pen?
K: Yes, Sam – here's a pen ... and a card.
S: Oh, okay... .

3 *S:* Have you got a phone card, Katy?
K: Yes, here you are. Do you know the dialling code for Sydney?
S: Yes – I've written it down. It's here. Padma will be really surprised to hear from us.
K: Let me speak to her after you, okay?

Unit 12, exercise 6

1 The sound of a plane landing and the pilot announcing, *Welcome to Heathrow, ladies and gentlemen ...*

2 The sound of newspaper pages being rustled and turned over and Katy saying *Oh, look at this ...*

3 The sound of water running in a shower and Sam lathering himself while singing: *"I'm getting married in the morning, la-la the sun is going to shine, I'm getting married, I'm getting married, so get .... "*

4 The organ music of the Wedding March in a church. Sam's voice whispering, *"Have you got the ring?"* And a male voice whispering back, *"Yes, here you are."* The vicar coughing and beginning the wedding service: *Dearly beloved, we are gathered here today ...*

DICTIONARY

Hier finden Sie sämtliche Wörter und Wendungen des Buches in alphabetischer Reihenfolge mit ihrer phonetischen Lautschrift und ihrer deutschen Übersetzung. Darüber hinaus enthält das *Dictionary* die Wörter der A1-Liste der European Language Certificates der WBT Weiterbildungs-Testsysteme GmbH , die für dieses Buch vorausgesetzt werden. Sie sind mit * markiert. Die Wörter, die Sie nur wieder erkennen sollen, wenn sie Ihnen begegnen, sind mit einer *kursiv gedruckten* Fundstelle markiert. Die Wörter, die als Lernvokabular vorgesehen sind, haben eine gerade gedruckte Fundstelle bei sich.

Die Fundstellen sind folgendermaßen zu lesen: die erste Ziffer weist auf die Unit hin, in der das Wort vorkommt. Die anschließende Zahl gibt die Nummer der Aufgabe an, in der das jeweilige Wort auftritt. Damit ist **accident** 7.2 also ein Wort, das in Unit 7 / Activity 2 zum ersten Mal vorkommt und zum Lernwortschatz gehört.

Die anderen Abkürzungen bedeuten:

H = Highlight
I = Introduction (= Wortschatz, der auf der Auftaktseite zu einer Unit erscheint)
IP = Ivor Problem-Seite
LC = Language and culture
S = Selfstudy
TT = Tourist Tip

Phonetische Lautschrift

englischer Laut		ähnlicher deutscher Laut
[ɪ]	in	*in*
[e]	yes	*fett*
[æ]	thanks	zwischen *a* und *ä*
[ʌ]	come	*machen*
[ɒ]	coffee	*Motte*
[ʊ]	look	*Butter*
[ə]	number	*singe*
[iː]	meet	*Knie*
[ɑː]	father	*Bahn*
[ɔː]	four	wie *o* in deutsch *Borke*
[uː]	too	*Buch*
[ɜː]	early	*Börse*
[eɪ]	day	nicht wie deutsch *ei* sondern [e] + [ɪ]
[aɪ]	nice	*Eile*
[ɔɪ]	boy	*heute*
[aʊ]	how	*Frau*
[əʊ]	no	[ə] + [ʊ]

englischer Laut		ähnlicher deutscher Laut
[ɪə]	here	*hier*
[eə]	where	*sehr*
[ʊə]	tourist	[ʊ] + [ə]
[v]	have	*Virus*
[θ]	thanks	wie ein gelispeltes *ss* in *Biss*
[ð]	this	wie ein gelispeltes *s* in *Sand*
[s]	seat	*Muße*
[z]	please	*Museum*
[ʃ]	she	*Schiff*
[ʒ]	television	*Regie*
[tʃ]	cheers	*klatschen*
[dʒ]	German	[d] + [ʒ]
[ŋ]	song	*singen*
[l]	old	hinten im Mund gesprochen
[j]	unit	*ja*
[w]	we	durch die Lippen gesprochen wie [uː]
[r]	repeat	vorn im Mund gesprochen

[ː] der vorangehende Laut wird lang gesprochen
['] Hauptbetonung: die folgende Silbe wird stark betont
[ˌ] Nebenbetonung: die folgende Silbe wird leicht betont

A

* **a.m. (ante meridiem)** [ˌeɪ‿'em (ˌæntɪ mə'rɪdɪəm)] vormittags, morgens 2.LC
* **a/an** [ə, æn, ən] ein/e 1.2
Aboriginal [ˌæbə'rɪdʒənl] *ursprünglich australisch 8.S1*
Aborigine [ˌæbə'rɪdʒəniː] *austral. Ureinwohner/in 7.S1*
about [ə'baʊt] über *1.8*, 2.2
* **about** [ə'baʊt] ungefähr 1.TT
* **above** [ə'bʌv] oben, oberhalb 2.7
abroad [ə'brɔːd] im/ins Ausland 7.9
absolutely ['æbsəluːtlɪ] absolut, total 11.7
accent ['æksnt] Akzent, Dialekt *5.LC*
accept [ək'sept] akzeptieren, annehmen 5.S1
* **accident** ['æksɪdənt] Unfall 7.2
accomodation [əˌkɒmə'deɪʃn] Unterbringung, Unterkunft 4.8
account [ə'kaʊnt]: **(bank) account** (Bank)Konto 1.7
ache (n.) [eɪk] Schmerz *IP.2*
across [ə'krɒs] (quer) über, durch 9.S1
act (out) [ækt (aʊt)] spielen, darstellen *11.1*
action ['ækʃn] Handlung *8.6*
active ['æktɪv] aktiv *H2*
activity [æk'tɪvətɪ] Aktivität, Unternehmung, Übung *1.5*
actor ['æktə] Schauspieler *H3*
actress ['æktrɪs] Schauspielerin *12.S1*
actual ['æktʃʊəl] echt, wirklich, tatsächlich 10.S4
actually ['æktʃʊəlɪ] eigentlich, wirklich 1.7
adaptor [ə'dæptə] Adapter *9.7*
add [æd] hinzufügen 6.5
* **address** [ə'dres] Adresse 5.2
adjective ['ædʒɪktɪv] Adjektiv, Eigenschaftswort *3.4*
adopt [ə'dɒpt] annehmen, übernehmen *4.LC*
adult ['ædʌlt] Erwachsene/r 9.S1
advance [əd'vɑːns]: **in advance** im Voraus 11.S5

adverb ['ædvɜ:b] Adverb *7.8*
advert ['ædvɜ:t] Anzeige, Werbung *9.2*
advertise ['ædvətaɪz] werben für, bewerben *8.LC*
advice [əd'vaɪs] Rat(schlag) *10.4*
afraid [ə'freɪd]: **I'm afraid** ich bedaure, leider 4.8
African ['æfrɪkən] afrikanische(r, s) *H3*
* **after** ['ɑ:ftə] nach, hinter 2.3: **after all** doch noch, letztendlich 12.2
* **afternoon** [ˌɑ:ftə'nu:n] Nachmittag 2.S5: * **in the afternoon** am Nachmittag, nachmittags 2.1; * **on Saturday afternoons** samstagnachmittags 11.S1
* **again** [ə'gen] noch einmal, wieder 1.4
age [eɪdʒ] Alter 8.2
agent ['eɪdʒənt]: **travel agent** Reisekaufmann, -frau *9.TT*
ago [ə'gəʊ] vor *(zeitlich)* 3.2
air [eə] Luft *12.9*
airline ['eəlaɪn] Fluglinie, -gesellschaft 5.2
airplane ['eəpleɪn] Flugzeug 12.9
* **airport** ['eəpɔ:t] Flughafen 1.I
alcohol ['ælkəhɒl] Alkohol 3.8
* **all** [ɔ:l] alle/s H1: * **all day** den ganzen Tag 6.2; * **all right** in Ordnung 1.3
allergy ['ælədʒɪ] Allergie *IP.2*
alligator ['ælɪgeɪtə] Alligator *7.S5*
* **allowed** [ə'laʊd]: **be allowed to** dürfen 3.LC
along [ə'lɒŋ] entlang *H1*
alphabet ['ælfəbet] Alphabet *8.1*
* **also** ['ɔ:lsəʊ] auch 2.LC
although [ɔ:l'ðəʊ] obwohl *H3*
altogether [ˌɔ:ltə'geðə] (alles) zusammen, insgesamt 4.8
* **always** ['ɔ:lweɪz] immer 1.S6
amazing [ə'meɪzɪŋ] erstaunlich, umwerfend 11.2
* **American** [ə'merɪkən] Amerikanisch; amerikanische(r, s); Amerikaner/in 3.10
amount [ə'maʊnt] Menge, Summe 10.S4
* **and** [ænd, ənd] und 1.I
angle ['æŋgl] Winkel *10.S1*
angry ['æŋgrɪ] ärgerlich 11.1
animal ['ænɪml] Tier *H2*
* **another** [ə'nʌðə] ein/e andere(r, s); ein/e weitere(r, s) 1.3
* **answer** ['ɑ:nsə] Antwort 1.7
answer ['ɑ:nsə] (be)antworten *1.8*: **answer the phone** ans Telefon gehen, abheben *5.9*
ant [ænt] Ameise *8.S1*
antelope ['æntɪləʊp] Antilope *H2*
* **any** ['enɪ] welche, irgendwelche 2.2
anybody ['enɪbɒdɪ] (irgend)jemand *7.TT*
* **anything** ['enɪθɪŋ] (irgend)etwas; alles 7.2: * **anything else?** noch etwas? 9.S4
anyway ['enɪweɪ] jedenfalls, sowieso 10.2
apartheid [ə'pɑ:thaɪd] Apartheit, Rassentrennung *H2*
apartment [ə'pɑ:tmənt] Apartment, Wohnung 10.S1
apology [ə'pɒlədʒɪ] Entschuldigung *IP.3*
apple ['æpl] Apfel *H1*, 6.3
appointment [ə'pɔɪntmənt] Termin, Verabredung *IP.2*
appropriate [ə'prəʊprɪət] angemessen, passend *11.LC*
April ['eɪprəl] April *2.5*
aquarium [ə'kweərɪəm] Aquarium *11.6*
architect ['ɑ:kɪtektʃə] Architektur *H1*
* **area** ['eərɪə] Gegend, Gebiet H1: **area code** *(AE)* Vorwahl *11.8*
around [ə'raʊnd] umher, herum *1.I*
arrival [ə'raɪvl] Ankunft *1.1*
* **arrive** [ə'raɪv] ankommen 1.I
arrow ['ærəʊ] Pfeil *5.S1*
art [ɑ:t] Kunst 2.S5
article ['ɑ:tɪkl] Artikel, Produkt *H1*
as [æz] wie *(Vergleich)* 1.S6; *hier:* wenn 9.S5: **as … as** (genau)so … wie *2.8*, 7.S1; **as long as** solange 6.2
ask (for) ['ɑ:sk (fə)] fragen (nach), bitten (um) 6.8
assistant [ə'sɪstənt] Verkäufer/in, Angestellte/r 10.2
associate [ə'səʊʃɪeɪt] assoziieren, verbinden *10.7*
* **at** [æt, ət] bei, an, auf 1.I: * **at 7 o'clock** um 7 Uhr 3.S4; * **at home** zu Hause, daheim 5.10; **at last** endlich 5.S3; **at least** zumindest, wenigstens 10.2; **at night** abends, nachts 2.1; **at once** auf einmal 5.S1; **be at one** eins sein, im Einklang sein *9.S1*; * **at work** in/bei der Arbeit 1.6
athlete ['æθli:t] Leichtathlet/in *H3*
attached [ə'tætʃt] beigefügt, angehängt 5.8
attack [ə'tæk] angreifen *H2*
attacker ['ətækə] Angreifer/in *H2*
attend [ə'tend] teilnehmen, anwesend sein *5.I*
attract [ə'trækt] anziehen, anlocken *H1*
attraction [ə'trækʃn] Attraktion, Sehenswürdigkeit *1.I*
aubergine ['ɔ:bəʒi:n] Aubergine *6.3*
audio-visual [ˌɔ:dɪəʊ'vɪʒʊəl] audiovisuell *3.2*
August ['ɔ:gəst] August 2.2
aunt [ɑ:nt] Tante 5.5
Australian [ɒ'streɪlɪən] australische(r, s); Australier/in *5.I*, 5.S1
* **Austrian** ['ɒstrɪən] österreichische(r, s); Österreicher/in 11.TT
authentic [ɔ:'θentɪk] authentisch, echt *2.2*
author ['ɔ:θə] Autor/in, Schriftsteller/in *H3*
autograph ['ɔ:təgrɑ:f] Autogramm *H1*
average ['ævərɪdʒ] durchschnittlich, Durchschnitts- *H1*
* **away** [ə'weɪ] weg, fort, entfernt 1.I
awful ['ɔ:fl] schrecklich 3.4

B

baboon [bə'bu:n] Pavian *H2*
* **back** [bæk] zurück 3.2
bacon ['beɪkən] (Frühstücks)Speck 6.3
* **bad** [bæd] schlecht, schlimm 3.5
badly-paid [bædlɪ'peɪd] schlecht bezahlt *H2*
* **bag** [bæg] Tasche 1.2
baggage *(AE)* ['bægɪdʒ] Gepäck *1.3*: **baggage reclaim** Gepäckausgabe *5.2*
bagpipes ['bægpaɪps] Dudelsack *1.S1*
baked [beɪkt] gebacken 6.S3
bakery ['beɪkərɪ] Bäckerei 2.1
balcony ['bælkənɪ] Balkon 9.4
ball [bɔ:l] Ball *H1*
ballet ['bæleɪ] Ballett *11.2*
balloon [bə'lu:nɪst] Ballon 8.2
banana [bə'nɑ:nə] Banane 10.6
* **bank** [bæŋk] Bank *(Geld)* 2.1
banquet ['bæŋkwɪt] Bankett *2.S1*
bar [bɑ:] Bar *3.9*
barbecue ['bɑ:bəkju:] Grill, Grillen, Grillfest 8.5
barbecued ['bɑ:bəkju:d] gegrillt *H3*
bargain ['bɑ:gən] Gelegenheitskauf, Schnäppchen *10.TT*
bathe [beɪð] baden 10.S1
* **bathroom** ['bɑ:θrʊm] Bad, Badezimmer, Toilette *(AE)* 7.LC
* **battery** ['bætərɪ] Batterie 10.2
* **be** [bi:] sein 1.S1
beach [bi:tʃ] Strand 6.S1
bean [bi:n] Bohne *H3*
beautiful ['bju:təfəl] (wunder)schön 1.S1
beauty ['bju:tɪ] Schönheit *H1*
because [bɪ'kəz] weil *1.1*, 6.S1
become [bɪ'kʌm] werden (zu) 3.S4
* **bed** [bed] Bett 9.3: **bed and breakfast** Frühstückspension 4.7
bedroom ['bedrʊm] Schlafzimmer 9.7
* **beer** [bɪə] Bier 2.8
beet [bi:t] Rübe *H3*
* **before** [bɪ'fɔ:] (be)vor, vorher 2.I
begin [bɪ'gɪn] beginnen, anfangen *1.9*, 2.9
beginning [bɪ'gɪnɪŋ] Anfang *5.3*
beginning [bɪ'gɪnɪŋ] beginnend *1.9*
behaviour [bɪ'heɪvjə] Benehmen, Verhalten *12.10*
* **behind** [bɪ'haɪnd] hinter 8.7
believe [bɪ'li:v] glauben 11.S4
belong (to) [bɪ'lɒŋ (tə)] gehören (zu), angehören *8.LC*
below [bɪ'ləʊ] unten, unter, unterhalb *1.6*, 8.7
beside [bɪ'saɪd] neben *3.2*
* **best** [best]: **the best** der/die/das beste 3.6
bet [bet] wetten 11.S1
* **between** [bɪ'twi:n] zwischen 2.LC
* **big** [bɪg] groß 2.S1
biking ['baɪkɪŋ] Radfahren *H2*
bikini [bɪ'ki:nɪ] Bikini 10.6
* **bill** [bɪl] Rechnung H1
billion ['bɪljən] Milliarde 11.S1

* **bird** [bɜːd] Vogel H1: **bird's-eye view** Vogelperspektive *5.I*
birth [bɜːθ] Geburt 8.4
* **bit** [bɪt]: **a bit** ein bisschen, ein wenig 1.S6
bite [ˌbaɪt]: **mosquito bite** Mückenstich *IP.2*
* **black** [blæk] schwarz 5.S4
Bless you! ['bles jʊ] Gesundheit! 12.8
block [blɒk] (Wohn-, Häuser)Block 10.S1
blond [blɒnd] blond *H3*
blood [blʌd] Blut 7.S1
* **blue** [bluː] blau 5.S4
board [bɔːd] Tafel *2.8*
board [bɔːd]: **on board** an Bord 2.S1
board [bɔːd] an Bord gehen, einsteigen 12.2: **boarding card** Bordkarte 4.S5
* **boat** [bəʊt] Boot, Schiff H1
bobsleigh ['bɒbsleɪ] Bob *H3*
boil [bɔɪl] kochen 6.2
* **book** [bʊk] Buch H1
book [bʊk] buchen, reservieren *H1*, 4.8
border ['bɔːdə] Grenze 4.S1
* **born** [bɔːn]: **be born** geboren werden/sein 3.S4
borrow ['bɒrəʊ] (aus)leihen, borgen 5.2
* **both** [bəʊθ] beide/s 1-7: **both ... and ...** sowohl ... als auch ... *1.LC*
* **bottle** ['bɒtl] Flasche 6.LC: **bottle shop** Spirituosenhandlung *6.LC*
box [bɒks] Kästchen *6.5*: **box office** Kartenschalter 11.S5
boyfriend ['bɔɪfrend] Freund *(eines Mädchens/einer Frau) 1.I*, 1.2
bracket ['brækɪt] Klammer *12.S1*
brain [breɪn] Gehirn *H2*
brake [breɪk] Bremse *IP.1*
* **bread** [bred] Brot H1: **bread roll** Brötchen 6.2
break [breɪk] (zer)brechen, kaputtgehen 8.2: **break down** kaputtgehen, zusammenbrechen 8.2
* **breakfast** ['brekfəst] Frühstück 6.3
breathtaking ['breθteɪkɪŋ] atemberaubend *H1*
breeding ['briːdɪŋ] Paarung *H2*
bride [braɪd] Braut *12.S1*
bridge [brɪdʒ] Brücke 5.I
briefcase ['briːfkeɪs] Aktentasche 12.2
* **bring** [brɪŋ] (mit)bringen 6.LC
British ['brɪtɪʃ] Britisch; britische(r, s); Brite, Britin *4.LC*
brochure ['brəʊʃə] Broschüre 11.S4
broken ['brəʊkən] kaputt 6.S5
bronze [brɒnz] Bronze *9.S1*
* **brother** ['brʌðə] Bruder 5.2
* **brown** [braʊn] braun 5.S4
buffalo ['bʌfələʊ] Büffel *H2*
build [bɪld] (er)bauen 7.4
* **building** ['bɪldɪŋ] Gebäude 2.9
bung *(austral.)* [bʌŋ]: **go bung** *(austral.)* kaputtgehen *8.2*
* **bus** [bʌs] Bus 1.7
bush [bʊʃ] Busch, Gebüsch 6.2
bushman ['bʊʃmən] Buschmann *H2*
business ['bɪznəs] Geschäft, Geschäfts- *1.LC*: **business card** Visitenkarte *11.LC*
businessman ['bɪznəsmæn] Geschäftsmann *H2*
* **but** [bʌt, bət] aber 1.I
button ['bʌtn] Knopf 10.2
* **buy** [baɪ] kaufen 3.LC
* **by** [baɪ] *hier:* bis, vor *(zeitlich)* 9.6; mit, per, von 2.S6
* **bye** [baɪ] tschüss 4.6
BYO (= bring your own) [ˌbiːwaɪ'əʊ] zum Selbermitbringen *6.LC*

C

cab *(AE)* [kæb] Taxi *4.LC*
cable car ['keɪbl kɑː] Kabinenbahn, Seilbahn *11.6*
* **café** ['kæfeɪ] Café 3.3
* **call** [kɔːl] Anruf 5.S1
* **call** [kɔːl] nennen 1.6; anrufen 2.9: **call out** heraus-/hinausrufen *2.8*
called [kɔːld] genannt, mit Namen *8.S4*
* **camera** ['kæmərə] Kamera, Fotoapparat 5.2
camp [kæmp] Lager *H2*
campaign [kæm'peɪn] Kampagne, Aktion *H1*
* **camping** ['kæmpɪŋ] Zelten 4.7
campsite ['kæmpsaɪt] Camping-, Zeltplatz *7.9*
* **can** [kæn, kən] können, kann(st), könnt 1.I
cancellation [ˌkænsə'leɪʃn] Kündigung, Sperrung *5.TT*
cancer ['kænsə] Krebs *H3*
capital ['kæpɪtl] Hauptstadt *H1*
* **car** [kɑː] Auto 1.2: * **car park** Parkplatz 1.2; **car rental** Autovermietung 8.2
* **card** [kɑːd] Karte 11.LC
care [keə] Versorgung, Fürsorge *11.S1*
* **careful** ['keəfəl] vorsichtig, aufmerksam 3.TT
Caribbean [ˌkærə'biːən] Karibik *H3*
carousel ['kærəsəl] Karussell *5.2*
* **carry** ['kærɪ] tragen 12.2
* **case** [keɪs] *hier:* Koffer 5.2
case [keɪs] Fall 7.2
* **cash** [kæʃ] Bargeld, bar 10.S4: **cash dispenser** Geldautomat 1.2; **cash machine** Geldautomat 1.3; **cash point** Bank-, Geldautomat 10.2
casino [kə'siːnəʊ] (Spiel)Kasino *H1*
castle ['kɑːsl] Burg, Schloss 2.2
catch [kætʃ] bekommen *(Zug, Erkältung)* 4.8
cathedral [kə'θiːdrəl] Kathedrale, Dom 2.2
Catholic ['kæθəlɪk] Katholik/in; katholisch 3.S4
cayenne pepper [keɪ'en ˌpepə] Cayennepfeffer *H3*
celery ['selərɪ] Sellerie 6.3
central ['sentrəl] zentral 9.2
* **centre** ['sentə] Zentrum, Mitte 1.S5
ceremonial [ˌserə'məʊnɪəl] zeremoniell, feierlich 12.S1
ceremony ['serəˌməʊnɪ] Zeremonie, Feierlichkeit *H1*
certain ['sɜːtn] gewiss, bestimmt *H1*
certainly ['sɜːtnlɪ] gewiss, natürlich, sicher(lich) 4.8
certificate [sə'tɪfɪkət] Zertificat, Auszeichnung *9.TT*: **certificate of vaccination** Impfpass *9.TT*
* **change** [tʃeɪndʒ] Wechselgeld 5.S1
* **change** [tʃeɪndʒ] wechseln, tauschen H.2; *hier:* umsteigen 4.8
character ['kærəktə] Charakter, Person *H3*
characteristic [ˌkæræktə'rɪstɪk] Charakteristikum, Eigenschaft, Eigenheit *H3*
charge [tʃɑːdʒ] Preis, Kosten 6.5
charge [tʃɑːdʒ]: **in charge** zuständig *IP.3*
chase [tʃeɪs] Verfolgungsjagd *H1*
chat [tʃæt] schwatzen, sich unterhalten *3.10*
* **cheap** [tʃiːp] billig 3.5
check *(AE)* [tʃek] Rechnung *H1*
check [tʃek] (über)prüfen *2.4*, 12.4: * **check in** einchecken, anmelden, aufgeben *(Gepäck)* 9.3
check-in ['tʃek‿ɪn] Einchecken, Abfertigung *12.2*
* **Cheers!** [tʃɪəz] Prost! 12.8
* **cheese** [tʃiːz] Käse 6.3
* **cheque** [tʃek]: **(by) cheque** (mit/per) Scheck *7.9*
* **chicken** ['tʃɪkɪn] Huhn, Hähnchen H2
* **child (children)** [tʃaɪld ('tʃɪldrən)] Kind 3.LC
Chinese [ˌtʃaɪ'niːz] Chinesisch; chinesische(r, s); Chinese, Chinesin 2.8
chips [tʃɪps] Pommes frites 6.2
choice [tʃɔɪs] Wahl, Auswahl 6.2
* **choose** [tʃuːz] (aus)wählen 3.5
* **Christmas** ['krɪsməs] Weihnachten 6.S1
* **church** [tʃɜːtʃ] Kirche 10.1
* **cigarette** [ˌsɪgə'ret] Zigarette 5.7
* **cinema** ['sɪnəmə] Kino 2.S5
circle ['sɜːkl] Kreis, Kringel *11.3*
citizen ['sɪtɪzn] (Staats)Bürger/in, Einwohner/in *H1*
* **city (cities)** ['sɪtɪ ('sɪtɪz)] (Groß-, Welt-) Stadt 1.S5: **city centre** Stadtmitte, City 1.S7
* **class** [klɑːs] Kurs, Klasse 1.1
classical music ['klæsɪkl ˌmjuːzɪk] Klassik, klassische Musik *H1*
* **clean** [kliːn] sauber 6.5
clear(ly) [klɪə(lɪ)] klar, deutlich 2.2
clever ['klevə] schlau, klug 10.S1
climate ['klaɪmɪt] Klima 6.S1
climb [klaɪm] Klettern, Aufstieg 6.2
climb [klaɪm] klettern, besteigen *5.I*, 7.2: **climbing** Klettern, Bergsteigen *H2*
clock [klɒk] Uhr *2.LC*
* **close** [kləʊz] schließen 2.9
close(ly) [kləʊs(lɪ)] nahe, eng, knapp 10.S1
closing time ['kləʊzɪŋ ˌtaɪm] Ladenschluss *2.1*

* **clothes** [kləʊðz] Kleidung, Kleider 5.2
cloud [klaʊd] Wolke *H2*
club [klʌb] Klub, Verein 2.S7
clue [klu:] Hinweis *H3*
coach [kəʊtʃ] Reisebus 11.S5
* **coat** [kəʊt] Mantel, Jacke 10.6
code [kəʊd] *hier:* Vorwahl *5.1*, 5.2
* **coffee** ['kɒfɪ] Kaffee 6.8
coin [kɔɪn] Münze 5.S1
coke [kəʊk] Cola 3.7
* **cold** [kəʊld] kalt 3.5
colleague ['kɒli:g] Kollege, Kollegin, Mitarbeiter/in *5.I*
collect [kə'lekt] (ein)sammeln *5.7*
colonial-style [kə'ləʊnɪəlˌstaɪl] im Kolonialstil *9.2*
colony ['kɒlənɪ] Kolonie *9.S1*
* **colour** ['kʌlə] Farbe 5.3
colourful ['kʌləfəl] bunt, farbenprächtig *9.I*
* **come** [kʌm] kommen 1.6
* **comfortable** ['kʌmfətəbl] bequem, komfortabel 3.4
communicate [kə'mju:nɪkeɪt] kommunizieren, sich verständigen *H2*
company ['kʌmpənɪ] Firma, Unternehmen 1.7
comparative [kəm'pærətɪv] Komparativ, 1. Steigerungsform *3.5*
compare [kəm'peə] vergleichen *1.7*
* **complain** [kəm'pleɪn] sich beklagen, sich beschweren 12.S5
complaint [kəm'pleɪnt] Klage, Beschwerde *IP.3*
complete [kəm'pli:t] vervollständigen *2.4*, 8.2
complete(ly) [kəm'pli:t(lɪ)] komplett, vollkommen *10.S5*
complicated ['kɒmplɪkeɪtɪd] kompliziert *8.4*
* **concert** ['kɒnsət] Konzert 2.2
concrete ['kɒnkri:t] Beton, Zement *H1*
condition [kən'dɪʃn] Bedingung 6.S1
conference ['kɒnfərəns] Konferenz, Sitzung *5.I*, 4.S5
confirm [kən'f3:m] bestätigen *12.TT*
* **Congratulations!** [kənˌgrætʃʊ'leɪʃnz] Herzlichen Glückwunsch! 12.8
conservation [ˌkɒnsə'veɪʃn] Erhaltung, Bewahrung, Schutz *H2*
continent ['kɒntɪnənt] Kontinent *2.LC*
continue [kən'tɪnju:] fortfahren, weitermachen *H2*
control [kən'trəʊl] kontrollieren *H2*
convenience [kən'vi:njəns] Bequemlichkeit, Annehmlichkeit *7.LC*: **public convenience** öffentliche Toilette *7.LC*
conversation [ˌkɒnvə'seɪʃn] Unterhaltung, Gespräch *4.8*
conversion [kən'v3:ʒn] Umrechnung *1.TT*
copy ['kɒpɪ] Kopie *5.8*
* **corner** ['kɔ:nə] Ecke 10.S5
correct [kə'rekt] korrigieren, berichtigen *1.7*
correct [kə'rekt] korrekt, richtig *6.3*, 6.5
cost [kɒst] (Un)Kosten 8.3
* **cost** [kɒst] kosten 8.2
could [kʊd] könnte(st/t/n), konnte(st/t/n) 2.2
count [kaʊnt] zählen 7.2
countable ['kaʊntəbl] zählbar *10.S3*
* **country (countries)** ['kʌntrɪ ('kʌntrɪz)] Land 1.S1
couple ['kʌpl] (Ehe)Paar, Pärchen 4.S1
* **course** [kɔ:s] Kurs 1.1
course [kɔ:s]: **of course** natürlich, selbstverständlich 1.S1
cousin ['kʌzn] Vetter, Kusine 5.5
cover (up) ['kʌvə (ʌp)] verdecken, zudecken *4.3*
crash [kræʃ] Unfall, Zusammenstoß *H2*
cream [kri:m]: **ice cream** Eiskrem 6.8
creator [kri:'eɪtə] Schöpfer/in, Erfinder/in *H3*
credit ['kredɪt] Kredit 10.S4: * **credit card** Kreditkarte 5.TT
cricket ['krɪkɪt] Kricket *H2*
cricketer ['krɪkətə] Kricketspieler/in *H3*
crime [kraɪm] Kriminalität, Gewalt *H1*
crisps [krɪsps] (Kartoffel)Chips 3.7
crocodile ['krɒkədaɪl] Krokodil *7.S5*
cross [krɒs] Kreuz *7.5*
cross (over) [krɒs (əʊvə)] überqueren 9.8
crossword ['krɒsw3:d] Kreuzworträtsel *9.7*
crowded ['kraʊdɪd] überfüllt *H1*
cruise [kru:z] Schifffahrt, Bootstour *11.6*
cry [kraɪ] weinen *H3*
cuisine [kʊɪ'zi:n] Küche *6.3*
cult [kʌlt] Kult *H3*
cultural ['kʌltʃərəl] kulturell 11.S1
culture ['kʌltʃə] Kultur *1.LC*, 10.S1
* **cup** [kʌp] Tasse 6.8
currency ['kʌrənsɪ] Währung 10.S4
curry ['kʌrɪ] Curry(gericht) 6.2
custom ['kʌstəm] Brauch, Sitte *6.TT*
customer ['kʌstəmə] Kunde, Kundin 4.S3
cycling ['saɪklɪŋ] Rad fahren 4.7

D

dad [dæd] Papa, Vati 1.2
daily ['deɪlɪ] täglich *7.8*
* **damaged** ['dæmɪdʒd] beschädigt 10.2
danger ['deɪndʒə] Gefahr *H2*
dangerous ['deɪndʒərəs] gefährlich 11.4
dark [dɑ:k] dunkel *H3*
* **date** [deɪt] Datum 2.4
* **daughter** ['dɔ:tə] Tochter 1.S6
* **day** [deɪ] Tag 1.7
deal [di:l] Handel, Angebot *H1*
* **dear** [dɪə] Liebe(r) ... *(Brief)* 11.7
* **dear** [dɪə]: **Oh dear!** Ach du liebe Zeit!, Du meine Güte! 6.5
death [deθ] Tod *10.LC*
December [dɪ'sembə] Dezember 2.7
decide [dɪ'saɪd] (sich) entscheiden *6.5*, 10.2
decision [dɪ'sɪʒn] Entscheidung 6.4
deer [dɪə] Wild, Rehe, Hirsche *H2*
define [dɪ'faɪn] definieren, erklären *10.7*
definitely ['defɪnɪtlɪ] ganz bestimmt, auf jeden Fall 12.9
degree [dɪ'gri:] Grad 7.S1
* **delayed** [dɪ'leɪd] verspätet 12.2
delicious [dɪ'lɪʃəs] köstlich, lecker 3.4
* **dentist** ['dentɪst] Zahnarzt, Zahnärztin 8.S2
depart [dɪ'pɑ:t] abfahren, verlassen 4.S6
department store [dɪ'pɑ:tmənt ˌstɔ:] Kaufhaus *H1*
* **departure** [dɪ'pɑ:tʃə] Abflug 12.2
deposit [dɪ'pɒzɪt] Kaution *8.TT*
describe [dɪ'skraɪb] beschreiben *3.4*
description [dɪ'skrɪpʃn] Beschreibung *6.3*
desert ['dezət] Wüste *6.S1*
design [dɪ'zaɪn] gestalten, entwerfen *H1*
designer [dɪ'zaɪnə] Gestalter/in *H1*
desk [desk] Schreibtisch 5.2
dessert [dɪ'z3:t] Dessert, Nachspeise 6.2
dessertspoon [dɪ'z3:tspu:n] Teelöffel *H3*
detail ['di:teɪl] Detail, Einzelheit 2.9
develop [dɪ'veləp] (sich) entwickeln, entstehen 8.S1
diagonal [daɪ'ægənəl] diagonal 10.S1
dial ['daɪəl] wählen *(Telefon)* 5.S1: **dial tone** Freizeichen *(Telefon)* 5.S1; **dialling code** Vorwahl *5.1*, 5.S2
dialect ['daɪəlɪkt] Dialekt *7.TT*
dialogue ['daɪəlɒg] Dialog, Gespräch *1.4*
diamond ['daɪəmənt] Diamant *H2*
diary ['daɪərɪ] Tagebuch *4.2*
dictate [dɪk'teɪt] diktieren *8.7*
dictation [dɪk'teɪʃn] Diktat *8.7*
* **dictionary** ['dɪkʃənrɪ] Wörterbuch 9.7
* **die** [daɪ] sterben 8.S1
difference ['dɪfrəns] Unterschied *2.LC*
* **different** ['dɪfrənt] andere(r, s); verschieden, anders 2.TT
* **difficult** ['dɪfɪkəlt] schwierig 3.5
digital ['dɪdʒɪtl] digital 5.2
dining out [ˌdaɪnɪŋ‿'aʊt] essen gehen, auswärts essen *6.1*
dining room ['daɪnɪŋ rʊm] Esszimmer, Speisesaal 2.S1
* **dinner** ['dɪnə] (warmes) Abendessen 2.S1
dinosaur ['daɪnəsɔ:] Dinosaurier *H1*
diplomat ['dɪpləmət] Diplomat/in, Botschafter/in *H1*
direct [daɪ'rekt] direkt 4.S4
direction [daɪ'rekʃn] Richtung 5.S1: **directions** *(Mz)* Wegbeschreibung *9.8*
* **dirty** ['d3:tɪ] schmutzig 6.5
disc [dɪsk] Scheibe 10.S4
discman ['dɪskmæn] Discman, tragbarer CD-Spieler 10.4
discount ['dɪskaʊnt] Rabatt, Ersparnis 8.2

discover [dɪ'skʌvə] entdecken 8.S1
discuss [dɪ'skʌs] diskutieren *6.6*
dish [dɪʃ] Gericht, Speise *6.3*
disk [dɪsk] Diskette 5.2
distillery [dɪ'stɪlərɪ] Destillerie, Brennerei *3.2*
disturb [dɪ'stɜːb] stören *H2*
divide [dɪ'vaɪd] aufteilen, trennen *2.8*
divorce [dɪ'vɔːs] Scheidung *H1*
dizzy ['dɪzɪ] schläfrig, benommen *IP.2*
* **do** [duː] tun, machen 1.4
* **doctor** ['dɒktə] Arzt, Ärztin 1.7
document ['dɒkjʊmənt] Dokument 5.2
dolphin ['dɒlfɪn] Delfin 11.6
door [dɔː] Tür *7.LC*, 10.S1: **next door** nebenan *IP.2*
double ['dʌbl] verdoppeln *12.4*
double ['dʌbl] doppelt, Doppel- 8.2: **double-barrelled name** Doppelname *12.LC*; **double-decker** Doppeldecker- 7.S1
* **down** [daʊn] hin-/herunter 8.8
dozen ['dʌzn] Dutzend 12.S4
dragon ['drægən] Drache *10.S1*
draw [drɔː] zeichnen *9.6*
dreadful ['dredfəl] furchtbar, schrecklich *IP.2*
* **dress** [dres] Kleid 10.6: **dress code** Kleidungsvorschrift *11.LC*
* **drink** [drɪŋk] Getränk 2.9
drink [drɪŋk] trinken 1.S1
* **drive** [draɪv] fahren *(Auto)* 1.S7
driver ['draɪvə] Fahrer/in *6.TT*
driving licence [ˌdraɪvɪŋ 'laɪsəns] Führerschein 8.2
drop [drɒp] fallen (lassen) 7.2
* **dry** [draɪ] trocken 2.S5
during ['djʊərɪŋ] während 2.S1
Dutch [dʌtʃ] niederländisch, holländisch *H1*

E

e.g. (= for example) [iː'dʒiː] zum Beispiel *6.1*
each [iːtʃ] jede(r, s) *1.9*, 11.S1: **each other** miteinander *H2*
* **early** ['ɜːlɪ] früh 2.S7
* **easy** ['iːzɪ] leicht, einfach 3.5
* **eat** [iːt] essen 1.S1
education [ˌedjʊ'keɪʃn] Erziehung, (Aus)Bildung 11.S1
effective [ɪ'fektɪv] wirkungsvoll, effektiv *IP.2*
* **egg** [eg] Ei 6.1
* **electrical** [ɪ'lektrɪkl] elektrisch 12.9
elegant ['elɪgənt] elegant 2.S1
elephant ['elɪfənt] Elefant *H2*
elevator *(AE)* ['elɪveɪtə] Lift, Aufzug *H1*
emblem ['embləm] Emblem, Wahrzeichen *H2*
emperor ['empərə] Kaiser *H3*
employ [ɪm'plɔɪ] anstellen, beschäftigen *H2*
* **empty** ['emptɪ] leer 5.2
en suite [en 'swiːt] (Bad) im Zimmer 9.3
end (in) [end (ɪn)] enden (auf) *11.3*
endless ['endləs] endlos, ewig *H1*
energetic [ˌenə'dʒetɪk] dynamisch, energievoll *H2*
engineer [ˌendʒɪ'nɪə] Ingenieur/in 1.S3
English ['ɪŋglɪʃ] Englisch; englische(r, s); Engländer/in 1.7: **English-speaking** englischsprachig *1.LC*, 7.5
enjoy [ɪn'dʒɔɪ] genießen, gefallen 1.I
enlarge [ɪn'lɑːdʒ] vergrößern *H2*
enormous [ɪ'nɔːməs] enorm, riesig 11.1
enter ['entə] eintreten, betreten 10.S1
entertain [ˌentə'teɪn] unterhalten 2.S1
entertainment [ˌentə'teɪnmənt] Unterhaltung *9.1*, 11.S1
enthusiastic [ɪnˌθjuːzɪ'æstɪk] enthusiastisch, begeistert, leidenschaftlich *H3*
epilepsy ['epɪlepsɪ] Epilepsie *7.2*
escalator ['eskəleɪtə] Rolltreppe 9.S6
establish [ɪ'stæblɪʃ] gründen 3.2
European [ˌjʊərə'piːən] europäische(r, s); Europäer/in *2.TT*
even ['iːvn] sogar, selbst *2.TT*, 6.S1
* **evening** ['iːvnɪŋ] Abend 2.S5: * **in the evening(s)** abends, am Abend 2.1
event [ɪ'vent] Veranstaltung *H3*
ever ['evə] jemals 7.3
* **every** ['evrɪ] jede(r, s) 1.S1
everybody ['evrɪbɒdɪ] jeder 9.S1
everyone ['evrɪwʌn] jeder *3.LC*
* **everything** ['evrɪθɪŋ] alles 12.2
exactly [ɪg'zæktlɪ] genau 3.10
example [ɪg'zɑːmpl]: **for example (e.g.)** zum Beispiel *1.LC*
excellent ['eksələnt] ausgezeichnet 2.S5
except for [ɪk'sept ˌfɔː] außer *11.3*
excited [ɪk'saɪtɪd]: **be excited** aufgeregt sein, sich freuen 12.8
exciting [ɪk'saɪtɪŋ] aufregend 7.2
exclusive [ɪk'skluːsɪv] exklusiv *H1*
* **excuse me** [ɪk'skjuːz ˌmiː] entschuldigen Sie / entschuldige 5.2
exercise ['eksəˌsaɪz] Übung, Aufgabe *7.6*
exhibition [ˌeksɪ'bɪʃn] Ausstellung 11.S5
exotic [ɪg'zɒtɪk] exotisch, ausgefallen *H1*
expect [ɪk'spekt] erwarten *6.TT*
* **expensive** [ɪk'spensɪv] teuer 3.4
experience [ɪk'spɪərɪəns] Erlebnis, Erfahrung 7.4
experience [ɪk'spɪərɪəns] erleben, erfahren 11.6
expert ['ekspɜːt] Experte, Expertin 8.2
* **explain** [ɪk'spleɪn] erklären, erläutern 4.S4
export ['ekspɔːt] Export(ware) *H3*
expression [ɪk'spreʃn] Ausdruck *11.8*
extra ['ekstrə] *hier:* Extra-, zusätzliche Ausgabe/Kosten 8.2
extra ['ekstrə] besonders, zusätzlich *11.LC*
extreme [ɪk'striːm] Extrem *6.S1*
extremely [ɪk'striːmlɪ] extrem, äußerst *6.TT*
eye [aɪ] Auge *5.I*

F

facility [fə'sɪlətɪ] Einrichtung *9.1*
fact [fækt] Fakt, Tatsache *7.S1*
factory ['fæktrɪ] Fabrik 11.6
fair [feə] fair, gerecht 11.S1
fall *(AE)* [fɔːl] Herbst *H1*
fall in love [ˌfɔːl‿ɪn 'lʌv] sich verlieben 4.S1
false [fɔːls] falsch *1.7*
familiar [fə'mɪljə] vertraut, bekannt *H1*
* **family** ['fæməlɪ] Familie 1.10: **family name** Familienname, Nachname 1.10; **family tree** (Familien)Stammbaum *5.6*
famous ['feɪməs] berühmt 2.2
fancy ['fænsɪ] Lust haben auf 2.7
fantastic [fæn'tæstɪk] fantastisch 1.7
* **far** [fɑː] fern, weit 9.4
farmer ['fɑːmə] Bauer, Farmer *H2*
fascinate ['fæsɪneɪt] faszinieren, anziehen, fesseln *H1*
fascination [ˌfæsɪ'neɪʃn] Faszination, Anziehungskraft *H1*
fashion ['fæʃn] Mode *H2*
* **fast** [fɑːst] schnell 7.TT
* **father** ['fɑːðə] Vater 4.S1
faulty ['fɔːltɪ] fehlerhaft, kaputt *10.2*
favourite ['feɪvrɪt] Lieblings- 6.8
feast [fiːst] Feste, Feier *12.S1*
February ['febrʊərɪ] Februar 3.2
fee [fiː] Gebühr 5.S1
* **feel** [fiːl] (sich) fühlen 5.LC
female ['fiːmeɪl] weiblich 5.5
* **ferry** ['ferɪ] Fähre 9.S1
festival ['festəvl] Festival, Feier 2.2
fever ['fiːvə] Fieber *9.TT*: **hay fever** Heuschnupfen *IP.2*
* **few** [fjuː]: **a few** einige, ein paar 7.6
fight [faɪt] Kampf, Streit *H2*
fight [faɪt] kämpfen, streiten *H3*
figure ['fɪgə] Figur *H3*
* **fill (in)** [fɪl (ɪn)] (aus)füllen 5.2
fill up [ˌfɪl‿'ʌp] tanken *IP.1*
film [fɪlm] Film 1.S7
film [fɪlm] filmen *H3*
final ['faɪnl] endgültig, letzte(r, s) 10.S6
finally ['faɪnəlɪ] schließlich, endlich 12.7
finance ['faɪnæns] finanzieren 11.S1
financial [faɪ'nænʃl] finanziell, Finanz- 10.S1
* **find** [faɪnd] finden 1.3: **find out** herausfinden *1.10*
* **fine** [faɪn] fein, schön, gut 1.2
finish ['fɪnɪʃ] (be)enden, fertig werden 7.4
* **fire** ['faɪə] Feuer, Brand H3
first [fɜːst]: **(at) first** zuerst *1.I*, 5.S1: **first floor** *(AE)* Erdgeschoss *H1*
* **fish** [fɪʃ] Fisch, Fische 3.10
fish [fɪʃ] fischen, angeln 9.S1
fisherman (fishermen) ['fɪʃəmən] Fischer 11.6
fishing ['fɪʃɪŋ] Fischen, Angeln *H2*: **fishing boat** Fischerboot 9.S1
fit [fɪt] passen *10.5*
fix [fɪks] reparieren *IP.1*

flag [flæg] Flagge, Fahne *H1*
flash [flæʃ] Blitz *9.LC*
* **flat** [flæt] Wohnung, Apartment 1.I
flea market ['fliː ˌmɑːkɪt] Flohmarkt *H1*
* **flight** [flaɪt] Flug 5.2: **flight attendant** Flugbegleiter/in, Steward/ess *6.6*
floor [flɔː] (Fuß)Boden; Stock(werk), Etage 9.7: **first floor** *(AE)* Erdgeschoss *H1*; * **ground floor** Erdgeschoss H1
flower ['flaʊə] Blume *H1*: **be in flower** blühen, in voller Blüte stehen *H2*
fluent ['fluːənt] flüssig, fließend 11.4
* **fly** [flaɪ] fliegen 1.S4
focus ['fəʊkəs] Fokus, Schwerpunkt *1.10*
fog [fɒg] Nebel 6.7
* **foggy** ['fɒgɪ] neblig 6.7
* **follow** ['fɒləʊ] (ver)folgen *2.9*, 4.S1
* **food** [fuːd] Essen 3.4
* **foot (feet)** [fʊt (fiːt)] Fuß *(Längenmaß)*, Fuß 1.TT
football ['fʊtbɔːl] Fußball 2.8
footprint ['fʊtprɪnt] Fußabdruck *H1*
* **for** [fɔː, fə] für, *hier:* nach 1.I
forbid [fə'bɪd] verbieten *12.TT*
forecast ['fɔːkɑːst] Vorhersage 6.2
forest ['fɒrɪst] Wald 6.S1
forever [fə'revə] ewig, für immer *H2*
* **forget** [fə'get] vergessen 6.2
form [fɔːm] Form, Gestalt *1.4*, 10.S4
* **form** [fɔːm] Formular 5.2
form [fɔːm] formen, bilden *9.7*
formal ['fɔːml] formell, förmlich *1.LC*
formation [fɔː'meɪʃn] Gebilde, Form, Gestalt *H1*
fortnight ['fɔːtnaɪt] zwei Wochen, 14 Tage *9.I*, 11.2
fragrant ['freɪgrənt] wohlriechend, aromatisch, duftend *9.S1*
Franco-American [ˌfræŋkəʊ ə'merɪkən] franko-amerikanisch *H1*
free [friː] befreien *H2*
free [friː] frei; *hier:* umsonst, gratis 1.S5
freedom ['friːdəm] Freiheit 2.5
freeway *(AE)* ['friːweɪ] Schnellstraße *H1*
French [frentʃ] Französisch; französische(r, s); Franzose, Französin 1.S6
frequency ['friːkwənsɪ] Häufigkeit *7.7*
fresh [freʃ] frisch 4.2
Friday ['fraɪdeɪ] Freitag 2.7
* **friend** [frend] Freund/in, Bekannte/r 1.LC
* **friendly** ['frendlɪ] freundlich 3.4
friendship ['frendʃɪp] Freundschaft *H1*
* **from** [frɒm, frəm] aus, von 2.2: * **I'm from** ich bin / komme aus 1.1; * **from ... to** von ... bis 2.S7
* **front** [frʌnt] Front, Vorderseite 10.S1: * **in front of** vor H1
* **fruit** [fruːt] Frucht, Früchte, Obst 10.6
fuel [fjʊəl] Treibstoff 8.2
* **full** [fʊl] voll 3.10
* **fun** [fʌn] Spaß 9.S1

further ['fɜːðə] weiter 9.S5
future simple [ˌfjuːtʃə 'sɪmpl] Futur I, Zukunft *(gramm.) 6.S1*
futuristic [ˌfjuːtʃə'rɪstɪk] futuristisch *9.S1*

G

gallery ['gælərɪ] Galerie 2.S5
gambling ['gæmblɪŋ] Glücksspiel *11.S1*: **gambling hall** Spielhalle *H1*
game [geɪm] Spiel *2.8*; *hier:* Wild *H2*
gap [gæp] Lücke *10.3*
* **garden** ['gɑːdn] Garten 9.2
garlic ['gɑːlɪk] Knoblauch *H3*
gas *(AE)* [gæs] Benzin 8.5
gate [geɪt] Gate, Tor, Flugsteig 12.2
gents *(Mz)* [dʒents] Herrentoilette *7.LC*
geographical [ˌdʒɪəʊ'græfɪkl] geografisch *H1*
German ['dʒɜːmən] Deutsch; deutsche(r, s); Deutsche/r 1.9: **in German** auf Deutsch 3.2
* **get** [get] bekommen, erhalten 1.9; *hier:* gelangen 5.10
get [get] *hier:* holen 3.7; *hier:* werden 9.7: **get married** heiraten 4.S1; * **get up** aufstehen 7.8
ghost [gəʊst] Geist, Gespenst *2.9*, 7.6
giant ['dʒaɪənt] riesig, Riesen- *11.6*
gift [gɪft] Geschenk 3.2
gin [dʒɪn] Gin 3.7
giraffe [dʒə'rɑːf] Giraffe *H2*
* **girl** [gɜːl] Mädchen 4.S1
girlfriend ['gɜːlfrend] Freundin *(eines Jungen/Mannes) 1.LC*, 5.2
* **give** [gɪv] geben 1.2
glad [glæd] froh 6.2
gladioli [ˌglædɪ'əʊlɪ] Gladiole *(Blume) H2*
* **glass** [glɑːs] Glas 3.7
* **glasses** ['glɑːsɪz]: **(a pair of) glasses** Brille 10.4
* **go** [gəʊ] gehen 1.I
going to ['gəʊɪŋ tə] werden *(Zukunft) 11.S1*, 11.S2
gold [gəʊld] Gold *H2*
goldfish ['gəʊldfɪʃ] Goldfisch *9.S1*
golf [gɒlf] Golf *2.S7*, 8.8: **golf course** Golfplatz *3.S1*
golf [gɒlf] Golf spielen, golfen *3.S1*
golfer ['gɒlfə] Golfer/in, Golfspieler/in *3.S1*
* **good** [gʊd] gut 1.7: **good luck** (viel) Glück *4.S5*, 12.7
* **goodbye** [ˌgʊd'baɪ] auf Wiedersehen 1.LC
goose (geese) [guːs (giːs)] Gans *12.S1*
government ['gʌvnmənt] Regierung 8.S1
governor ['gʌvənə] Gouverneur *H3*
granddaughter ['grændɔːtə] Enkelin 5.S6
grandfather ['grændfɑːðə] Großvater 5.5
grandmother ['grænmʌðə] Großmutter 10.S5
* **great** [greɪt] großartig 1.3

great-grandparents [ˌgreɪt'grændpeərənts] Urgroßeltern *H3*
* **green** [griːn] grün 5.S4
greet [griːt] (be)grüßen *1.LC*
grey [greɪ] grau 5.2
grid [grɪd] Gitter, Tabelle *2.6*
grilled [grɪld] gegrillt *H3*
grocery store ['grəʊsərɪ ˌstɔː] Lebensmittelladen 9.S2
groom [gruːm] Bräutigam *12.S1*
ground [graʊnd] Grund, Gebiet, Boden *H2*: * **ground floor** Erdgeschoss H1
* **group** [gruːp] Gruppe 3.LC
guard [gɑːd] Wächter/in, Aufseher/in 12.4
guess [ges] (er)raten *7.6*
* **guest** [gest] Gast 7.S6
* **guide** [gaɪd] Führer/in 7.4
guided ['gaɪdɪd] geführt, mit (Reise)Führung *2.9*
guys [gaɪz] Leute, Kerle, Typen *H2*

H

haggle ['hægl] Handel, Handeln, Feilschen *10.S6*
haggle ['hægl] handeln, feilschen 10.5
* **hair** [heə] Haar/e 12.2
hairdresser ['heədresə] Frisör/in *6.TT*
hairdryer ['heədraɪə] Fön 9.7
hairstyle ['heəstaɪl] Frisur *H3*
* **half** [hɑːf] halb, Hälfte 3.7: * **half an hour** eine halbe Stunde 10.S5
* **hand** [hænd] Hand 1.LC
hand (over) [hænd ('əʊvə)] (über)geben, reichen 8.2
handbag ['hændbæg] Handtasche 8.S5
handmade ['hændmeɪd] handgemacht 11.6
handprint ['hændprɪnt] Handabdruck *H1*
handset ['hændset] Hörer *5.S1*
happen ['hæpən] passieren, geschehen 10.2
* **happy** ['hæpɪ] glücklich 12.8
harbour ['hɑːbə] Hafen *5.I*, 9.S1
hard [hɑːd] schwer, hart 11.2: **Hard luck!** Das war Pech! Pech gehabt! 12.8
hat [hæt] Hut 12.S5
* **have** [hæv] haben; nehmen, essen, trinken 6.2
have to ['hæv tə] müssen *4.S4*, 5.2
hay fever ['heɪ ˌfiːvə] Heuschnupfen *IP.2*
* **he** [hiː] er 1.1
head [hed] Kopf *11.LC*
headache ['hedeɪk] Kopfschmerzen 7.2
heading ['hedɪŋ] Überschrift *8.4*
health [helθ] Gesundheit 7.2
* **hear** [hɪə] hören 3.7
heart [hɑːt] Herz *7.2*: **heart attack** Herzinfarkt *8.S1*
* **heavy** ['hevɪ] schwer 1.2
hectic ['hektɪk] hektisch 10.S1
height [haɪt] Höhe *1.TT*

helicopter ['helɪkɒptə] Hubschrauber, Helikopter *7.S5*
hell [hel] Hölle *5.2*
* **hello** [hə'ləʊ] Hallo. Guten Tag. Grüß' Gott. 1.1
* **help** [help] Hilfe 7.TT
* **help** [help] helfen H1
helpful ['helpfʊl] hilfreich, hilfsbereit 8.6
* **her** [hɜː] ihr/e; ihr, sie *(Objekt)* 1.I
* **here** [hɪə] hier 1.7: * **here you are** hier, bitte; bitte schön 11.8
heritage ['herɪtɪdʒ] Erbe, Tradition *2.9*
hers [hɜːz] ihre(r,s) 5.2
* **herself** [hɜː'self] sie (sich) selbst 4.6
* **Hi** [haɪ] Hallo! 1.3
* **high** [haɪ] hoch 1.S1
highlands ['haɪləndz] Hochland, Berge *H3*
highlight ['haɪlaɪt] Höhepunkt *H1*
highway *(AE)* ['haɪweɪ] Autobahn, Schnellstraße *8.5*
hilly ['hɪlɪ] hügelig, steil *H1*
* **him** [hɪm] ihm, ihn .12
* **himself** [hɪm'self] er sich selbst 4.6
hippo ['hɪpəʊ] Nilpferd, Flusspferd *H2*
hire ['haɪə] mieten, leihen *5.I*, *7.9*
* **his** [hɪz] sein/e, seine(r,s) 4.5
history ['hɪstərɪ] Geschichte 4.2
* **hobby** ['hɒbɪ] Hobby, Zeitvertreib 11.2
hold [həʊld] halten 5.9: **hold on** in der Leitung bleiben, „dran" bleiben *(Telefon)* 5.9
hole [həʊl] Loch 3.S1
* **holiday(s)** ['hɒlədeɪ(z)] Urlaub, Ferien 1.I
* **home** [həʊm] Heim, Zuhause H1: * **at home** zu Hause, daheim 5.10
* **hope** [həʊp] hoffen 5.2: **I hope so.** Das hoffe ich. 5.2
horizontally [ˌhɒrɪ'zɒntəlɪ] horizontal, waagrecht *10.7*
horse [hɔːs] Pferd 11.S1: **horse racing** Pferderennen 11.S1; **horse-riding** Reiten *H2*
* **hospital** ['hɒspɪtl] Krankenhaus 1.7
host [həʊst] Gast *6.TT*
* **hot** [hɒt] heiß 3.5
hot-air balloon [hɒtˌeə bə'luːn] Heißluftballon *5.I*
* **hotel** [həʊ'tel] Hotel 2.8
* **hour** ['aʊə] Stunde 2.LC
* **house** [haʊs] Haus H1
How are you? [haʊ 'ɑː ˌjuː] Wie geht es dir/Ihnen/euch? 1.2
How do you do? [ˌhaʊ djʊ 'duː] Wie geht es dir/Ihnen/euch? *(Begrüßungsformel)* 1.6
however [haʊ'evə] jedoch *11.TT*
huge [hjuːdʒ] riesig *H1*
* **hungry** ['hʌŋgrɪ] hungrig 8.S5
hunt [hʌnt] jagen *H2*
* **hurt** [hɜːt] (sich) verletzen, schmerzen 4.6
* **husband** ['hʌzbənd] Ehemann 1.S6

I

* **I** [aɪ] ich 1.1
ice [aɪs] Eis 3.8: **ice cream** Eiskrem 6.8
icon ['aɪkn] Ikone, Vorbild *H2*
* **idea** [aɪ'dɪə] Idee, Vorstellung, Gedanke 1.2
ideal [aɪ'dɪəl] ideal *H2*
identification [aɪˌdentɪfɪ'keɪʃn] Identifikation 5.S1
if [ɪf] wenn, falls, ob *2.3*, 4.8
image ['ɪmɪdʒ] Bild *H1*
immigrant ['ɪmɪgrənt] Immigrant/in, Einwanderer, Einwanderin *H1*
* **important** [ɪm'pɔːtnt] wichtig 5.2
impossible [ɪm'pɒsəbl] unmöglich 11.2
impressive [ɪm'presɪv] eindrucksvoll, beeindruckend *H2*
* **in** [ɪn] in 1.I: **in charge** zuständig *IP.3*
* **inch** [ɪntʃ] Inch, Zoll *(Längenmaß)* 1.TT
including [ɪn'kluːdɪŋ] einschließlich 2.S1
incoming ['ɪnkʌmɪŋ] eingehend 5.S1
independence [ˌɪndɪ'pendəns] Unabhängigkeit 2.5
* **Indian** ['ɪndɪən] Indianer/in H1; Indisch; indische(r, s); Inder/in 2.S5
indicate ['ɪndɪkeɪt] anzeigen, kennzeichnen *12.LC*
industry ['ɪndəstrɪ] Industrie *H1*
influence ['ɪnflʊəns] beeinflussen *H1*
informal [ɪn'fɔːml] informell, formlos *1.LC*
* **information** [ˌɪnfə'meɪʃn] Information, Auskunft 1.9: **tourist information centre** Fremdenverkehrsbüro, Touristeninformation 8.8
inhabitant [ɪn'hæbɪtənt] Einwohner/in *H2*, *9.S1*
initial [ɪ'nɪʃl] Initiale, Anfangsbuchstabe *H1*
injection [ɪn'dʒekʃn] Spritze, Injektion *9.TT*
insert [ɪn'sɜːt] einwerfen *5.S1*
instead [ɪn'sted] stattdessen 10.4
* **insurance** [ɪn'ʃʊərəns] Versicherung 8.2
insured [ɪn'ʃʊəd] versichert 8.2
* **interested** ['ɪntrəstɪd]: **be interested in** sich interessieren für 1.S7
* **interesting** ['ɪntrəstɪŋ] interessant 2.2
* **international** [ˌɪntə'næʃnl] international 1.1
interpreter [ɪn'tɜːprɪtə] Übersetzer/in, Dolmetscher/in 1.7
* **into** ['ɪntə] in ... hinein H1
introduce ... to [ˌɪntrə'djuːs tʊ] ... vorstellen *1.1*, 1.S2
introduction [ˌɪntrə'dʌkʃn] Einführung, Vorstellung *1.6*
iron ['aɪən] Eisen, Bügeleisen *9.7*
* **island** ['aɪlənd] Insel 1.S1
islander ['aɪləndə] Inselbewohner/in, Insulaner/in *H3*
* **it** [ɪt] es 1.2
* **Italian** [ɪ'tæljən] Italienisch; italienische(r, s); Italiener/in 1.S6
italics [ɪ'tælɪks]: **in italics** kursiv *8.6*
item ['aɪtəm] Gegenstand, Objekt *3.8*
ivory ['aɪvərɪ] Elfenbein *H2*

J

* **jacket** ['dʒækɪt] Jacke, Jackett 10.6
Jamaican [dʒə'meɪkən] jamaikanisch, Jamaikaner/in *H3*
January ['dʒænjʊərɪ] Januar *2.5*
Japanese [ˌdʒæpə'niːz] Japanisch; japanische(r, s); Japaner/in *3.2*
jerked [dʒɜːkt] mariniert, eingelegt *H3*
jewellery ['dʒuːəlrɪ] Schmuck *11.6*
* **job** [dʒɒb] Arbeit, Stelle 1.7
jogging ['dʒɒgɪŋ]: **go jogging** joggen *H1*
join (up) [dʒɔɪn ('ʌp)] verbinden *3.5*
journey ['dʒɜːnɪ] Fahrt, Reise 4.8
* **juice** [dʒuːs] Saft 10.6
July [dʒʊ'laɪ] Juli *2.5*, 11.S1
jump [dʒʌmp] springen *H2*
June [dʒuːn] Juni 6.S1
* **just** [dʒʌst] nur, einfach, gerade 1.LC

K

kangaroo [ˌkæŋgə'ruː] Känguru *6.2*
keep [kiːp] (be)halten, bewahren 12.S1
* **key** [kiː] Schlüssel 5.2
kick [kɪk] Tritt *H2*
kill [kɪl] töten *H2*
* **kilometre** *(BE)* ['kɪləˌmiːtə] Kilometer H1
kilt [kɪlt] Kilt, Schottenrock 1.S1
* **kind** [kaɪnd] Art, Sorte 4.7
kind [kaɪnd] nett, freundlich *9.S4*
king [kɪŋ] König *3.S5*
kiwi ['kiːwiː] Kiwi *6.1*
* **knife (knives)** [naɪf] Messer 12.2
* **know** [nəʊ] kennen, wissen 1.S1

L

label ['leɪbl] Anhänger, Etikett *12.6*
* **lady** ['leɪdɪ] Dame 7.LC
lager ['lɑːgə] Bier, Helles 3.8
* **lake** [leɪk] See 1.S1
* **lamb** [læm] Lamm 6.3
land [lænd] Land *6.S1*
* **land** [lænd] landen 12.S6
landlord ['lændlɔːd] Pächter, Vermieter *3.LC*
landmark ['lændmɑːk] Wahrzeichen, Meilenstein *H2*
landscape ['lænskeɪp] Landschaft 6.S1
* **language** ['læŋgwɪdʒ] Sprache, Sprach- 1.10
large [lɑːdʒ] groß 3.8
* **last** [lɑːst] letzte(r, s) 3.1: **at last** endlich 5.S3; * **last name** Nachname 8.2
* **late** [leɪt] spät, verspätet 4.8
Latin ['lætɪn] lateinisch, Latein *H3*
lavatory ['lævətrɪ] Waschraum, Toilette *7.LC*
law [lɔː] Gesetz, Recht 12.S1
lead [liːd] führen, leiten *H3*
leader ['liːdə] Führer/in 2.S1
leaf (leaves) [liːf (liːvz)] Blatt, Laub *H2*
leaflet ['liːflɪt] Broschüre *3.2*
* **learn** [lɜːn] lernen 1.S6
least [liːst]: **at least** zumindest, wenigstens 10.2

* **leave** [liːv] weggehen, -fahren 2.S3: **leave out** auslassen, weglassen *12.8*
lecture ['lektʃə] Vortrag, Vorlesung 5.2: **give a lecture** einen Vortrag halten 5.2
* **left** [left] (nach) links 8.7: * **on your left** links von dir/Ihnen/euch 8.8
legal ['liːgl] legal 11.S1
legalised ['liːgəlaɪzd] legalisiert, erlaubt *H1*
lemon ['lemən] Zitrone 3.7
leopard ['lepəd] Leopard *H2*
less [les] weniger *H2*
let [let] lassen 1.6
* **letter** ['letə] Buchstabe, Brief 6.1
letterbox ['letəbɒks] Briefkasten 11.8
level ['levl] Ebene 12.2
liberal ['lɪbərəl] liberal, nicht streng *H1*
liberty ['lɪbətɪ] Freiheit 7.2
library ['laɪbrərɪ] Bücherei, Bibliothek 2.1
licensed ['laɪsənst] lizenziert *6.LC*
life (lives) [laɪf (laɪvz)] Leben *7.6*, 12.S1
* **lift** [lɪft] Lift, Aufzug 12.2
lift [lɪft] (ab-hoch)heben 5.S1
* **light** [laɪt] Licht 10.S5
light [laɪt] leicht 12.9
lightning ['laɪtnɪŋ] Blitz *6.S1*
* **like** [laɪk] mögen, gern haben 1.7: * **I would like (= I'd like)** ich möchte/hätte gerne 3.7
* **like** [laɪk] (so) wie 1.S1
lily ['lɪlɪ] Lilie *H2*
limit ['lɪmɪt] Grenze, Begrenzung 8.2
limit ['lɪmɪt] begrenzen, einschränken 8.S1
line [laɪn] Linie, Zeile, Strich *1.9*, 10.S1
liner [laɪnə] Kreuzer *9.S1*
link [lɪŋk] Verbindung, Verknüpfung 12.7
lion ['laɪən] Löwe *H2*
list [lɪst] Liste *11.1*
* **listen (to)** ['lɪsn (tə)] (zu)hören 1.6
* **litre** ['liːtə] Liter 3.TT
little ['lɪtl] *hier:* wenig *H3*: * **a little** ein bisschen 10.1
* **live** [lɪv] leben, wohnen *1.9*
live [laɪv] lebend, lebendig 12.S1
local ['ləʊkl] örtlich, lokal, Orts- *2.1*, 4.2
location [ləʊ'keɪʃn] Ort *8.2*
loch [lɒk] See *(schott.) 1.S1*
log on [lɒg‿'ɒn] sich einloggen *H1*
* **long** [lɒŋ] lang 1.7
loo *(colloq.)* [luː] Klo *7.LC*
* **look** [lʊk] Blick 10.2: * **have a look (at)** einen Blick werfen (auf), ansehen 10.2
* **look (at)** ['lʊk‿ət] (an)schauen, (aus)sehen 1.10: * **look after** achten auf, sich kümmern um 4.6; * **look for** suchen 12.2; * **look forward to** sich freuen auf 1.2
look-alike ['lʊkəlaɪk] Doppelgänger/in, Imitator/in *H1*
lorry (lorries) ['lɒrɪ] Lieferwagen, Lastwagen 8.5
lose [luːz] verlieren *5.TT*, 8.6
lot [lɒt]: **a lot** viel, oft 1.S1; * **a lot (of) / lots of** viel/e 1.7
love [lʌv] Liebe; Alles Liebe, Liebe Grüße *(Briefschluss)* 3.S5: **fall in love** sich verlieben 4.S1
love [lʌv] lieben 1.7
lovely ['lʌvlɪ] nett, toll 1.2
low [ləʊ] niedrig, wenig 3.8
luck [lʌk]: **good luck** (viel) Glück *4.S5*, 12.7; **Hard luck!** Das war Pech! Pech gehabt! 12.8
luckily ['lʌkɪlɪ] zum Glück *H2*
* **lucky** ['lʌkɪ]: **be lucky** Glück haben 5.TT
* **luggage** ['lʌgɪdʒ] Gepäck 1.2
* **lunch** [lʌntʃ] Mittagessen 2.S5
* **lunchtime** ['lʌntʃˌtaɪm] Mittagszeit 9.3
luxury ['lʌkʃərɪ] Luxus 9.S1

M

* **machine** [mə'ʃiːn] Maschine, Gerät, Apparat 10.7
magazine [ˌmægə'ziːn] Magazin, Zeitschrift *H1*
magnificent [mæg'nɪfɪsnt] herrlich, prächtig *H3*
maiden ['meɪdn] Jungfrau *12.LC*: **maiden name** Mädchenname *12.LC*
mail *(AE)* [meɪl] Post 11.8
mailbox *(AE)* ['meɪlbɒks] Briefkasten 11.8
main [meɪn] Haupt- *H1*, 3.8: **main course** Hauptgericht 6.2
mainland ['meɪnlænd] Festland *11.TT*
major ['meɪdʒə] groß, größer; Haupt- 6.7
make [meɪk] machen, tun, bilden *2.5*, 3.S1: **make it** es schaffen 12.2; **make notes/a note** sich Notiten/eine Notiz machen, etw. notieren *2.TT*; **make sure** sichergehen, sich vergewissern *5.TT*, 11.S1; **make up** erfinden, sich ausdenken *4.1*
making ['meɪkɪŋ] Herstellung 3.2
malaria [mə'leərɪə] Malaria *9.TT*
male [meɪl] männlich 5.5
malt [mɔːlt] Malz *3.2*
* **man (men)** [mæn (men)] Mann 4.S1
manner ['mænə] Art und Weise *11.3*
* **many** ['menɪ] viele 1.S1
* **map** [mæp] (Land)Karte, Stadtplan 2.8
March [mɑːtʃ] März *2.5*
marinade ['mærɪneɪd] Marinade *H3*
marital status ['mærɪtl ˌsteɪtəs] Familienstand *8.4*
mark [mɑːk] kennzeichnen, markieren *9.8*
* **market** ['mɑːkɪt] Markt 9.8
marriage ['mærɪdʒ] Ehe 12.S1
* **married** ['mærɪd] verheiratet 1.S6
marry ['mærɪ] heiraten 4.S1
marvellous ['mɑːvələs] ausgezeichnet 3.4
massacre ['mæsəkə] massakrieren, abschlachten, metzeln *H1*
massive ['mæsɪv] massiv, riesig *9.S1*
match [mætʃ] zuordnen *1.S3*
matching ['mætʃɪŋ] passend, zugehörig *6.7*, 10.S2
matinée ['mætɪneɪ] Nachmittagsvorstellung *11.S5*
matter ['mætə]: **it doesn't matter** es ist egal, es macht nichts aus *5.LC*
maximum ['mæksɪməm] Maximum, maximal, Höchst- *1.TT*
May [meɪ] Mai 9.S4
may [meɪ] könnte vielleicht *7.LC*, *9.7*
maybe ['meɪbiː] vielleicht 4.S1
mayonnaise [ˌmeɪə'neɪz] Majonäse 6.3
* **me** [miː] ich, mich, mir 1.2
* **meal** [miːl] Mahlzeit 5.I
meaning ['miːnɪŋ] Bedeutung *1.3*
measure ['meʒə] Maß, Maßeinheit *3.TT*
* **meat** [miːt] Fleisch 6.2
medal ['medl] Medaille *H3*
medical ['medɪkl] medizinisch *5.I*, 11.S1
* **medicine** ['medsɪn] Medizin *IP.2*
* **meet** [miːt] kennen lernen, treffen 1.I
member ['membə] Mitglied, Teilnehmer/in *1.9*
memorial [mə'mɔːrɪəl] Denkmal *H1*
memory ['memərɪ] Erinnerung, Gedächtnis *2.8*
mend [mend] reparieren, ausbessern *IP.1*
mention ['menʃn] erwähnen *H1*
* **menu** ['menjuː] Speisekarte 3.10
mess [mes] Unordnung, Chaos 12.2
message ['mesɪdʒ] Nachricht, Mitteilung, Botschaft 5.10
messiah [mə'saɪə] Messias *H3*
* **metal** ['metl] Metall 10.S4
* **metre** ['miːtə] Meter 1.S1
metric system [ˌmetrɪk 'sɪstəm] Dezimalsystem *1.TT*
microphone ['maɪkrəfəʊn] Mikrofon *H2*
midday [ˌmɪd'deɪ] Mittag *2.LC*, 2.S7
* **midnight** ['mɪdnaɪt] Mitternacht 2.LC
might [maɪt] könnte vielleicht *8.4*
mild [maɪld] mild 6.S1
* **mile** [maɪl] Meile 7.S1
mileage ['maɪlɪdʒ] Meilenzahl *8.2*
* **million** ['mɪljən] Million H1
mind [maɪnd] Sinn, Geist, Gedanken *H1*
mine [maɪn] Mine *H2*
mine [maɪn] meine(r,s) 5.7
minestrone [ˌmɪnɪ'strəʊnɪ] Gemüsesuppe, Minestrone *6.2*
minimum ['mɪnɪməm] Minimum, minimal, Mindest- *5.S1*
* **minute** ['mɪnɪt] Minute 1.7
miss [mɪs] Fräulein *H1*
miss [mɪs] verpassen, verfehlen *H1*, 7.4
* **mistake** [mɪ'steɪk] Fehler 6.5
mix [mɪks] Mischung *H2*
mix [mɪks] mischen *1.S3*
mixture ['mɪkstʃə] Mischung 10.S1

mobile phone [ˌməʊbaɪl ˈfəʊn] Mobiltelefon, Handy 1.9
model [ˈmɒdl] Modell *10.2*
modern [ˈmɒdən] modern 9.S1
* **moment** [ˈməʊmənt] Moment, Augenblick 4.8
Monday [ˈmʌndeɪ] Montag 2.7
* **money** [ˈmʌnɪ] Geld H1: **make money** Geld verdienen *H1*
monolith [ˈmɒnəlɪθ] Monolith *8.S1*
monster [ˈmɒnstə] Monster, Ungeheuer 2.2
* **month** [mʌnθ] Monat 2.4
monument [ˈmɒnjʊmənt] Monument, Denkmal *H2*
* **more** [mɔː] mehr, weitere 7.S1: **no more** kein/e mehr, nicht mehr 5.S1
* **morning** [ˈmɔːnɪŋ] Morgen, Vormittag 2.S7: **in the morning(s)** morgens, am Morgen *2.1*
mosquito bite [məsˈkɪːtəʊ ˌbaɪt] Mückenstich *IP.2*
* **most** [məʊst]: **(the) most** (der/die/das) meiste 1.S1; **mostly** meistens, hauptsächlich *H2*
* **mother** [ˈmʌðə] Mutter 1.LC
motorbike [ˈməʊtəbaɪk] Motorrad 7.5
motorway [ˈməʊtəweɪ] Autobahn, Schnellstraße 8.5
* **mountain** [ˈmaʊntɪn] Berg 1.S1: **the mountains** Gebirge, die Berge 9.S1
movie theater *(AE)* [ˈmuːvɪ ˌθɪətə] Kino *H1*
* **Mr** [ˈmɪstə] Herr *(Anrede)* 9.S4
* **Ms** [ˈmɪsɪz] Frau *(Anrede für Frauen unabhängig vom Familienstand)* 9.S4
* **much** [mʌtʃ] viel 1.S1: **how much is/are** wie viel kostet/kosten 9.S6
multi-racial [ˌmʌltɪˈreɪʃl] gemischtrassig, Vielvölker- *H2*
mum [mʌm] Mama, Mutti 1.2
museum [ˌmjuːˈzɪəm] Museum 1.7
mushroom [ˈmʌʃrʊm] Pilz 6.3
* **music** [ˈmjuːzɪk] Musik 2.2
musical [ˈmjuːzɪkl] musikalisch 1.S7
must [mʌst] Muss 9.S1
* **must** [mʌst] müssen 9.6
mustn't (must not) [(ˈmʌsnt) mʌst ˈnɒt] nicht dürfen 5.S1
* **my** [maɪ] mein/e 1.1
* **myself** [maɪˈself] ich mir/mich selbst 4.2

N

name [neɪm]: **my name's** ich heiße *1.1*
* **name** [neɪm] (be)nennen 8.S1
nation [ˈneɪʃn] Nation, Volk *H2*
national [ˈnæʃənl] national 2.5: **national park** Nationalpark *H1*
native [ˈneɪtɪv] ursprünglich, eingeboren *7.TT*: **native speaker** Muttersprachler/in *7.TT*
natural [ˈnætʃərəl] natürlich, Natur- *H1*
nature [ˈneɪtʃə] Natur 9.S1
* **near** [nɪə] nahe, in der Nähe von 1.2
nearby [nɪəˈbaɪ] in der Nähe 8.S1
nearly [ˈnɪəlɪ] fast, nahezu *H1*, 11.2
necessary [ˈnesəsərɪ] nötig, notwendig *9.7*
* **need** [niːd] brauchen, benötigen 1.2
negative [ˈnegətɪv] negativ, verneint, verneinend *2.3*
neighbour [ˈneɪbə] Nachbar/in 12.S1
neighbouring [ˈneɪbərɪŋ] benachbart, Nachbar- *H2*
nephew [ˈnefjuː] Neffe 5.5
nervous [ˈnɜːvəs] nervös 7.2
* **never** [ˈnevə] nie(mals) H1
* **new** [njuː] neu 1.7
newly-built [ˈnjuːlɪbɪlt] neugebaut *10.S1*
newsagent's [ˈnjuːzˌeɪdʒənts] Kiosk, Zeitschriftenhändler/in 8.S5
* **newspaper** [ˈnjuːsˌpeɪpə] Zeitung 7.8
* **next** [nekst] nächste(r, s) 1.5: * **next to** neben 1.1; **next door** nebenan *IP.2*
* **nice** [naɪs] nett, schön 1.6
* **night** [naɪt] Nacht 2.S3: **at night** abends, nachts 2.1
* **no** [nəʊ] nein 1.2
no-one [ˈnəʊwʌn] niemand *H1*
* **nobody** [ˈnəʊbədɪ] niemand, keiner 12.2
non-European [ˌnɒnjʊərəˈpiːən] nicht-europäische(r, s) *11.LC*
non-smoking [ˌnɒnˈsməʊkɪŋ] Nichtraucher- 4.8
none [nʌn] keine(r, s) 10.1
noodle [ˈnuːdl] Nudel 6.3
normal [ˈnɔːml] normal *1.LC*
* **north** [nɔːθ] Norden, Nord- 4.S1
Norwegian [nɔːˈwiːdʒən] norwegisch; Norweger/in *H3*
* **not** [nɒt] nicht 1.4: **not yet** noch nicht 8.S5
note [nəʊt]: **(bank) note** Geldschein, Banknote 10.S4
* **note** [nəʊt] Notiz 2.9: **make notes/a note** sich Notiten/eine Notiz machen, etw. notieren *2.TT*
* **nothing** [ˈnʌθɪŋ] nichts 10.2
noun [naʊn] Nomen, Substantiv *3.4*
November [nəʊˈvembə] November *2.5*
* **now** [naʊ] jetzt, nun 1.2
nowadays [ˈnaʊədeɪz] heutzutage *12.TT*
* **number** [ˈnʌmbə] Nummer, (An)Zahl *2.9*
number [ˈnʌmbə] nummerieren *3.7*
nut [nʌt] Nuss *6.1*
née [neɪ] Geborene *(bei Namen)* *12.LC*

O

* **o'clock** [əˈklɒk] Uhr (Zeitangabe) 2.S3: * **at 7 o'clock** um 7 Uhr 3.S4
object [ˈɒbdʒɪkt] Objekt, Gegenstand 12.2
occasionally [əˈkeɪzənəlɪ] manchmal 7.2
occupation [ˌɒkjʊˈpeɪʃn] Beruf *8.4*
ocean [ˈəʊʃn] Ozean, Meer 9.S1
* **of** [ɒv, əv] von 1.l
of course [əv ˈkɔːs] natürlich, selbstverständlich 1.S1
off licence [ˌɒf ˈlaɪsəns] Spirituosenhandlung *H2*
offer [ˈɒfə] Angebot 4.8
offer [ˈɒfə] (an)bieten *10.4*
officer [ˈɒfɪsə] Beamte/r *12.S1*
official [əˈfɪʃl] offiziell, amtlich, Amts- *9.LC*
* **often** [ˈɒfn] oft 1.S1
* **oil** [ɔɪl] Öl H2
* **old** [əʊld] alt 1.7
Olympic [əˈlɪmpɪk] olympisch *H3*: **Olympic Games** Olympische Spiele *H3*
on [ɒn]: **be on** stattfinden, auf dem Programm stehen *2.2*
* **on your left/right** [ˌɒn jɔː ˈleft/ˈraɪt] links/rechts von dir/Ihnen/euch 8.8
* **once** [wʌns] einmal, einst E2: **at once** auf einmal 5.S1
* **one** [wʌn] *(Stützwort)* 8.2
one [wʌn]: **be at one** eins sein, im Einklang sein *9.S1*
one-way ticket *(AE)* [ˈwʌnweɪ ˈtɪkɪt] Einzelfahrkarte *4.LC*
* **only** [ˈəʊnlɪ] nur 1.LC
* **only** [ˈəʊnlɪ] einzige(r, s) 11.S1
onto [ˈɒntə] auf hinauf, in hinein *12.TT*
* **open** [ˈəʊpn] öffnen 2.1
* **open** [ˈəʊpən] offen, geöffnet 2.9
open-air [əʊpnˈeə] Freiluft- *H1*
opening times [ˈəʊpənɪŋ ˌtaɪmz] Öffnungszeiten *2.1*, 3.2
opera [ˈɒprə] Oper *H1*
opposite [ˈɒpəzɪt] Gegenteil *3.5*
opposite [ˈɒpəzɪt] gegenteilig, entgegengesetzt *3.5*
* **opposite** [ˈɒpəzɪt] gegenüber E2
* **or** [ɔː] oder 1.7
orange [ˈɒrɪndʒ] Orange, Apfelsine 10.6
orchestra [ˈɔːkɪstrə] Orchester *H1*
orchid [ˈɔːkɪd] Orchidee *H2*
order [ˈɔːdə] Reihenfolge *3.7*; Bestellung *6.4*; **out of order** außer Betrieb *IP.3*
order [ˈɔːdə] bestellen *3.7*, 5.S3
organise [ˈɔːgənaɪz] organisieren 2.S1
originally [əˈrɪdʒənəlɪ] ursprünglich 3.S1
ostrich [ˈɒstrɪtʃ] Strauß *(Tierart)* *6.2*
* **other** [ˈʌðə] andere(r, s) 1.9
* **ours** [ˈaʊəz] unsere(r,s) 5.2
* **ourselves** [aʊəˈselvz] wir (uns) selbst 4.2
* **out of** [ˈaʊt‿əv] aus, heraus, *hier:* von H2: **out of order** außer Betrieb *IP.3*
outside [ˌaʊtˈsaɪd] draußen, außerhalb *9.LC*
* **over** [ˈəʊvə] über; her-, hinüber 4.S1; über, mehr als H1: **over there** da/dort drüben 12.2
overlook [ˌəʊvəˈlʊk] überschauen, Aussicht haben über *H2*
own [əʊn] eigene(r, s) *6.LC*
owner [ˈəʊnə] Besitzer/in, Eigentümer/in *3.LC*

P

* **p.m. (post meridiem)** [ˌpiː‿ˈem (ˌpəʊst məˈrɪdɪəm)] nachmittags, abends 2.LC
pack [pæk] (ein)packen 5.4

package ['pækɪdʒ] Packung, Paket 4.7
packet ['pækɪt] Paket, Päckchen 3.7
* **page** [peɪdʒ] Seite 1.10
painful ['peɪnfʊl] schmerzhaft 8.S5
painting ['peɪntɪŋ] Bild, Gemälde 4.2
* **pair** [peə] Paar 4.9
panda ['pændə] Panda(bär) *11.6*
panorama [ˌpænə'rɑːmə] Panorama *11.6*
panoramic [ˌpænə'ræmɪk] Panorama- *9.S1*
* **paper** ['peɪpə] Papier 3.5
paradise ['pærədaɪs] Paradies 9.S1
paragraph ['pærəgrɑːf] Absatz *12.7*
parcel ['pɑːsl] Päckchen 11.8
* **Pardon?** ['pɑːdn] Wie bitte? 5.2
* **parents** ['peərənts] Eltern 1.I
* **park** [pɑːk] Park 2.8
parkland ['pɑːklænd] Parkgelände *11.6*
part [pɑːt] Teil *1.6*, 2.S5
particular(ly) [pə'tɪkjʊlə(lɪ)] speziell, besonders, jeweilig 10.S4
partner ['pɑːtnə] Partner/in *1.1*
* **party** ['pɑːtɪ] Party, Fest, Feier 4.S3
passenger ['pæsɪndʒə] Fahrgast, Passagier/in *12.TT*
* **passport** ['pɑːspɔːt] (Reise)Pass 5.TT
past [pɑːst] Vergangenheit *4.5*: **past simple** einfache Vergangenheit *(gramm.) 4.S1*
past [pɑːst] an ... vorbei 11.6; nach (Uhrzeit) 2.S3: **half past three** halb vier 2.1
path [pɑːθ] Weg, Pfad 8.S1
* **pay** [peɪ] (be)zahlen 4.S4
payment ['peɪmənt] Bezahlung 5.S1
payphone ['peɪfəʊn] Münztelefon 5.S1
peace [piːs] Frieden *H2*
peak [piːk] Spitze, Gipfel 9.S1
peanut ['piːnʌt] Erdnuss 3.8
pelican ['pelɪkən] Pelikan *H2*
penguin ['peŋgwɪn] Pinguin *H2*
* **people** ['piːpl] Leute, Menschen 1.8
* **pepper** ['pepə] Pfeffer H2
per [pə] pro, je 9.4
percent [pə'sent] Prozent 7.S1
perfect ['pɜːfɪkt] perfekt 11.6
performance [pə'fɔːməns] Veranstaltung, Vorstellung 11.S5
* **perhaps** [pə'hæps] vielleicht 3.S1
permanent ['pɜːmənənt] permanent, ständig 8.4
* **person** ['pɜːsən] Person 1.1
personal ['pɜːsənl] persönlich *H2*
personality [ˌpɜːsə'nælətɪ] Persönlichkeit *8.LC*
* **petrol** ['petrəl] Benzin *IP.1*
phew [fjuː] puh 12.2
* **phone** [fəʊn] anrufen 2.2: **phone card** Telefonkarte 5.S1
* **photo** ['fəʊtəʊ] Foto 2.2: **take photos** fotografieren 4.2
photocopy ['fəʊtəʊˌkɒpɪ] Fotokopie *5.TT*
* **photograph** ['fəʊtəgrɑːf] Fotografie 5.5
photographer [fə'tɒgrəfə] Fotograf/in 11.6
phrase [freɪz] Phrase, Redewendung *1.4*
piano [pɪ'ænəʊ] Klavier *H1*
pickup ['pɪkʌp] Abholung 8.2
pick up [pɪk_'ʌp] abholen 5.8; aufheben, (zur Hand) nehmen *H3*
* **picture** ['pɪktʃə] Bild 8.S1
* **piece** [piːs] Stück, Teil 1.9
pilau ['piːlaʊ] Pilaw *6.2*
pink [pɪŋk] rosa, pink 11.6
* **pint** [paɪnt] Pint *(Hohlmaß)* 3.8
pirate ['paɪərət] Pirat *H3*
* **place** [pleɪs] Ort 2.2
plan [plæn] Plan *H2*
* **plan** [plæn] planen 8.TT
* **plane** [pleɪn] Flugzeug 2.LC
plant [plɑːnt] Pflanze *H1*
plantation [plɑːn'teɪʃn] Plantage *H2*
plate [pleɪt] Schild *8.LC*
* **play** [pleɪ] spielen 1.S1
player ['pleɪə] Spieler/in 3.S1
playground ['pleɪgraʊnd] Spielplatz *H1*
pleasant ['pleznt] angenehm, freundlich 11.S1
* **please** [pliːz] bitte 1.6
pleased to meet you [ˌpliːzd tə 'miːt jʊ] angenehm; nett, Sie/dich/euch kennen zu lernen 1.6
plural ['plʊərəl] Plural, Mehrzahl *5.4*
pocket ['pɒkɪt] Tasche *(Kleidung) 1.10*, 12.2
point [pɔɪnt] Punkt 7.S1
police [pə'liːs] Polizei *H2*: **police station** Polizeistation, -wache 8.S5
* **policeman (policemen)** ['pəliːsmən] Polizist 9.LC
polite [pə'laɪt] höflich *2.3*, 11.1
political(ly) [pə'lɪtɪkl(ɪ)] politisch *H2*
politician [ˌpɒlɪ'tɪʃn] Politiker/in *H1*
pool [puːl] Pool, Schwimmbecken, -bad 7.8
poor [pɔː] arm 3.5
popular ['pɒpjʊlə] beliebt *11.6*, 11.S1
population [ˌpɒpjʊ'leɪʃn] Bevölkerung, Einwohnerzahl 7.S1
positive ['pɒzətɪv] positiv *2.3*
possible ['pɒsəbl] möglich 2.S1
* **post** [pəʊst] Post H1: * **post office** Postamt 2.1
post [pəʊst] schicken, senden 8.S5
* **postcard** ['pəʊstkɑːd] Postkarte 4.2
* **potato (potatoes)** [pə'teɪtəʊ (pə'teɪtəʊz)] Kartoffel 6.2
practise ['præktɪs] üben *6.8*
prawn [prɔːn] Garnele *6.2*
prediction [prɪ'dɪkʃn] Vorhersage, Voraussagung *6.6*
prefer [prɪ'fɜː] vorziehen, lieber mögen *4.7*
prescription [prɪ'skrɪptʃn] (Arzt-)Rezept *IP.2*
present ['preznt] Geschenk *10.8*
present perfect [ˌpreznt 'pɜːfɪkt] Perfekt *(gramm.) 7.6*
present progressive [ˌpreznt prə'gresɪv] *Verlaufsform der Gegenwart (gramm.) 12.4*
present simple [ˌpreznt 'sɪmpl] Präsens, Gegenwart *1.S1*
presentation [ˌprezn'teɪʃn] Präsentation 3.2
president ['prezɪdənt] Präsident/in *H1*
press [pres] drücken *2.9*, 10.2
pretty ['prɪtɪ] hübsch 3.5
prevent [prɪ'vent] verhindern 12.S1
* **price** [praɪs] Preis H1
prince [prɪns] Prinz *3.S4*
prison ['prɪzn] Gefängnis *H1*
prisoner ['prɪznə] Gefangene/r, Häftling *H2*
* **private** ['praɪvət] privat 2.S1
prize [praɪz] Preis *(Gewinn) H2*
probably ['prɒbəblɪ] wahrscheinlich *1.TT*, 5.2
* **problem** ['prɒbləm] Problem E.2
produce [prə'djuːs] her-, erstellen, produzieren 6.S1
project ['prɒdʒekt] Projekt 11.S1
Protestant ['prɒtɪstənt] Protestant/in; protestantisch 3.S4
* **pub** [pʌb] Gasthof, Kneipe 2.1
* **public** ['pʌblɪk] öffentlich 3.4: **public convenience** öffentliche Toilette *7.LC*; **public transport** öffentliche Verkehrsmittel 3.4
* **pullover** ['pʊləʊvə] Pullover 5.S8
punctual ['pʌŋktʃʊəl] pünktlich 11.S4
purse [pɜːs] Handtasche *H1*
put [pʊt] setzen, legen, stellen 1.2
puzzle ['pʌzl] Rätsel, Puzzle *H1*
puzzle ['pʌzl] verwirren, überraschen *H2*
pyramid ['pɪrəmɪd] Pyramide *1.5*

Q

quality ['kwɒlətɪ] Qualität 10.S6
* **quarter** ['kwɔːtə]: **(a) quarter** (ein) Viertel 2.S3
queen [kwiːn] Königin 2.S1
* **question** ['kwestʃən] Frage 1.8
questionnaire [ˌkwestʃə'neə] Fragebogen 7.2
queue [kjuː] Schlange stehen, anstehen 12.2
quick [kwɪk] schnell *3.LC*, 11.2
* **quiet** ['kwaɪət] ruhig, still, leise 11.1
quite [kwaɪt] ziemlich 10.1

R

race [reɪs] Rennen 11.S1
racecourse ['reɪskɔːs] Rennbahn *11.S1*
racial ['reɪʃl] Rassen- *H2*
* **radio** ['reɪdɪəʊ] Radio 10.4
radiologist [ˌreɪdɪ'ɒlədʒɪst] Radiologe, Radiologin *1.7*
* **rain** [reɪn] Regen 6.S1: **rain forest** Regenwald 6.S1
* **rain** [reɪn] regnen 1.S1
rainbow ['reɪnbəʊ] Regenbogen *H2*
rainy ['reɪnɪ] regnerisch, verregnet *2.S5*
range [reɪndʒ] Kette, Zug *H2*

rarely ['reəlɪ] selten *7.7*
rate [reɪt] Preis(kategorie) 4.8; *hier:* Rate, Zahl *H1*
raw [rɔː] roh 6.3
react [rɪ'ækt] reagieren *2.7*
* **read** [riːd] lesen 1.4: **read out** vorlesen *1.4*, *7.2*
* **ready** ['redɪ] bereit, fertig 6.2
* **really** ['rɪəlɪ] wirklich 1.S6
reasonable ['riːznəbl] vernünftig 9.2: **reasonably-priced** preislich vernünftig 9.2
receive [rɪ'siːv] erhalten, bekommen *H2*
recently ['riːsntlɪ] kürzlich, neulich *H1*
* **reception (desk)** [rɪ'sepʃn (desk)] Rezeption, Empfang 9.7
receptionist [rɪ'sepʃənɪst] Person am Empfang *9.4*
recognise ['rekəgnaɪz] erkennen 5.8
record ['rekɔːd] Aufzeichnung *9.TT*; Rekord *H1*
record [rɪ'kɔːd] berichten, aufzeichnen 7.S1
* **red** [red] rot 5.S4
redskin ['redskɪn] „Rothaut" *H1*
regards *(Mz)* [rɪ'gɑːdz] Grüße 11.2
regulation [ˌregjʊ'leɪʃn] Regelung 8.S1
relation [rɪ'leɪʃn] Verwandtschaft *5.6*
relax [rɪ'læks] sich entspannen 12.2
religion [rɪ'lɪdʒən] Religion, Glaube *H3*
remarry [riː'mærɪ] noch einmal heiraten 12.S1
* **remember** [rɪ'membə] sich erinnern an 1.1
remind [rɪ'maɪnd] erinnern 12.9
* **rent** [rent] (ver)mieten 8.2
rental ['rentl]: **car rental** Autovermietung 8.2
repair [rɪ'peə] Reparatur *10.2*
* **repair** [rɪ'peə] reparieren *IP.1*
repairer('s) [rɪ'peərə(z)] Reparateur/in, Werkstatt 10.2
* **repeat** [rɪ'piːt] wiederholen 1.S2
replace [rɪ'pleɪs] ersetzen *3.10*
report [rɪ'pɔːt] Bericht *6.7*
report [rɪ'pɔːt] melden, berichten 5.2
represent [ˌreprɪ'zent] vertreten, repräsentieren, verkörpern *H1*
representative [ˌreprɪ'zentətɪv] Angestellte/r, Vertreter/in 5.2
request [rɪ'kwest] Bitte, Wunsch *8.2*
request [rɪ'kwest] wünschen *8.2*
requirement [rɪ'kwaɪəmənt] Anforderung 9.S4
reservation [ˌrezə'veɪʃn] Reservierung 8.2; Schutzgebiet *H2*
reserve [rɪ'zɜːv] reservieren 4.8
resident ['rezɪdənt] Einwohner/in *H1*
resort [rɪ'zɔːt] Urlaubs-, Erholungort 8.S1
rest [rest] Rest *1.1*
* **restaurant** ['restərɒnt] Restaurant 2.5
result [rɪ'zʌlt] Ergebnis *8.6*
return [rɪ'tɜːn] zurückgeben, zurückkehren 5.S1: **return ticket** Rückfahrkarte 4.8

revolving [rɪ'vɒlvɪŋ] (sich) drehend *11.6*
rhino ['raɪnəʊ] Nashorn *H2*
rice [raɪs] Reis 6.2
rich [rɪtʃ] reich 3.5
ride [raɪd] Fahrt, Flug 9.S1
ride [raɪd] fahren 4.S1
* **right** [raɪt] in Ordnung, okay 7.2; richtig 1.7: * **all right** in Ordnung 1.3
* **right** [raɪt] (nach) rechts 8.8: * **on the right** rechts, auf der rechten Seite 8.8
ring [rɪŋ] *hier:* anrufen 5.S1; klingeln 5.10
* **river** ['rɪvə] Fluss 3.2
* **road** [rəʊd] Straße, Fahrbahn 8.TT
roadsign ['rəʊdsaɪn] Straßenschild *9.LC*
roast [rəʊst] gebraten, Brat- 6.2
rock [rɒk] Fels 8.S1
roll [rəʊl]: **bread roll** Brötchen 6.2
Roman ['rəʊmən] Römer/in; römisch *3.S4*
romance [rəʊ'mæns] Romantik *12.9*
* **room** [ruːm] Zimmer, Raum 9.3
round [raʊnd] Runde *3.LC*
round [raʊnd] rund 10.S4
round [raʊnd] herum, umher *1.9*: **round trip ticket** *(AE)* Rückfahrkarte *4.LC*
route [ruːt] Route, Weg, Strecke *9.8*
routine [ruː'tiːn] Routine, Tagesablauf *7.8*
row [rəʊ] Reihe *11.5*
royal ['rɔɪəl] königlich 2.S1
rugby ['rʌgbɪ] Rugby *H2*
rule [ruːl] Regel, Vorschrift *8.TT*
rum [rʌm] Rum *H3*
run [rʌn] laufen, rennen 4.S1; *hier:* fahren 9.S2
Russian ['rʌʃən] Russisch; russische(r, s), Russe, Russin 6.S6

S

sacred ['seɪkrɪd] heilig 8.S1
sad [sæd] traurig 12.9
safety ['seɪftɪ] Sicherheit *7.2*, 8.S1
sail [seɪl] segeln 9.S1
* **salad** ['sæləd] Salat H1
salt [sɔːlt] Salz *H3*
* **same** [seɪm]: **(the) same** (der/die/das)selbe; gleich 1.S6
sandal ['sændl] Sandale 10.6
Saturday ['sætədeɪ] Samstag 2.7
sauce [sɔːs] Soße 6.2
sausage ['sɒsɪdʒ] Wurst 6.3
save [seɪv] sparen 1.7
* **say** [seɪ] sagen 1.3: **say goodbye** sich verabschieden *1.LC*
scenery ['siːnərɪ] Landschaft, Gegend 3.4
* **school** [skuːl] Schule 2.1
scissors *(Mz)* ['sɪzəz] Schere 12.2
Scot [skɒt] Schotte, Schottin 1.S1
Scotch [skɒtʃ] Scotch (Whisky) 3.2
Scottish ['skɒtɪʃ] Schottisch; schottische(r, s); Schotte, Schottin 1.7
sea [siː] Meer 9.4
seafood ['siːfuːd] Meeresfrüchte 6.2

seal [siːl] Robbe, Seehund *H2*
seaman ['siːmən] Seemann *H3*
search [sɜːtʃ] Suche *10.7*
search [sɜːtʃ] durchsuchen *H2*
season ['siːzn] Jahreszeit, Saison 6.S1
* **seat** [siːt] Sitz(platz) 4.8: **seat belt** Sicherheitsgurt *8.TT*
security [sɪ'kjʊərətɪ] Sicherheit 12.4
* **see** [siː] sehen 1.2
select [sə'lekt] auswählen 8.2
selection [sə'lekʃn] Auswahl 8.2
self help [self 'help] Selbsthilfe *4.S3*
self-catering [ˌself'keɪtərɪŋ] Selbstversorgung, -verpflegung *4.7*
self-employed [ˌself‿ɪm'plɔɪd] selbstständig *4.S3*
* **self-service** [ˌself'sɜːvɪs] Selbstbedienung(s-) 3.10
selfstudy ['selfstʌdɪ] Selbststudium *1.S1*
* **sell** [sel] verkaufen 3.TT
* **send** [send] senden, schicken 4.S5
sensitive ['sensɪtɪv] sensibel, vorsichtig *11.LC*
sentence ['sentəns] Satz *1.4*
* **September** [sep'tembə] September 9.S4
sequoia tree [sɪ'kwɔɪə ˌtriː] Mammutbaum *H1*
serious ['sɪərɪəs] ernst(haft) *IP.1*
serve [sɜːv] servieren, bedienen *3.LC*, 4.S3
* **service** ['sɜːvɪs] Dienst, Service H1: **service station** Tankstelle *IP.1*
set free [set 'friː] freilassen *H1*
settler ['setlə] Siedler/in *H1*
several ['sevrəl] einige, mehrere *H1*
sex [seks] Geschlecht 8.S3
shake [ʃeɪk] schütteln *1.LC*: **shake hands** die Hand geben, Hände schütteln *1.LC*
share [ʃeə] teilen *H3*
sharp [ʃɑːp] scharf, spitz 12.2
* **she** [ʃiː] sie 3.3
sheet of paper ['ʃiːt‿əv 'peɪpə] Blatt/Stück Papier 10.S4
sheriff ['ʃerɪf] Sheriff *H3*
ship [ʃɪp] Schiff *H3*
shirt [ʃɜːt] Hemd *H2*
* **shoe** [ʃuː] Schuh 10.S6
shoot [ʃuːt] (er)schießen *H3*
* **shop** [ʃɒp] Laden, Geschäft 3.2
shopkeeper ['ʃɒpkiːpə] Ladeninhaber/in 10.S4
shopoholic [ˌʃɒpə'hɒlɪk] Kaufsüchtige/r *H1*
* **shopping** ['ʃɒpɪŋ]: **go shopping** einkaufen gehen 3.S5
* **short** [ʃɔːt] kurz 1.4
shorten ['ʃɔːtn] verkürzen, abkürzen *8.5*
shorts *(Mz)* [ʃɔːts] Shorts, kurze Hosen 5.4
should [ʃʊd] sollen, sollte(st/n/t) *1.LC*, 8.S2
shoulder ['ʃəʊldə] Schulter *9.LC*, 12.2
* **show** [ʃəʊ] Show, Vorführung H1
* **show** [ʃəʊ] zeigen 3.2
* **shower** ['ʃaʊə] Dusche 9.3

shuttle ['ʃʌtl] Zubringer 12.2
*__sick__ [sɪk] übel, krank 12.9
sickness ['sɪknəs]: **travel sickness** Reisekrankheit *IP.2*
sight [saɪt] Sehenswürdigkeit *9.I*
*__sightseeing__ ['saɪtˌsiːɪŋ] Sehenswürdigkeiten ansehen 4.7
sign [saɪn] Schild, Zeichen, Signal *6.6*
signature ['sɪgnətʃə] Unterschrift 8.S3
silk [sɪlk] Seide *H2*
similar ['sɪmɪlə] ähnlich *1.3*
simple ['sɪmpl] einfach *3.LC*: **simple past** einfache Vergangenheit *(gramm.) 7.S5*
simplify ['sɪmplɪfaɪ] vereinfachen *11.6*
since [sɪns] seit 8.S1
single ['sɪŋgl] unverheiratet, alleinstehend 8.4; Einzel- 4.8
singular ['sɪŋgjʊlə] Singular, Einzahl 10.6
Sir [sɜː] mein Herr *(Anrede)* 5.2
*__sister__ ['sɪstə] Schwester 5.5
*__sit__ [sɪt] sitzen, sich setzen 9.7
site [saɪt] Ort, Stelle 7.9
situation [ˌsɪtjʊ'eɪʃn] Situation *1.LC*
*__size__ [saɪz] Größe 10.S6
skeleton ['skelɪtn] Skelett *H1*
ski [skiː] Schi 2.S7
ski [skiː] Schi fahren 1.S1
skin [skɪn] Haut *H3*
sky [skaɪ] Himmel 11.6
skyline ['skaɪlɪnə] Skyline 9.S1
slave [sleɪv] Sklave, Sklavin *H3*
*__sleep__ [sliːp] schlafen 12.S5
sleepy ['sliːpɪ] schläfrig *IP.2*
slot [slɒt] Schlitz *5.S1*
*__slow__ [sləʊ] langsam 11.1
slum [slʌm] Elendsviertel *H3*
*__small__ [smɔːl] klein 3.S1
smile [smaɪl] lächeln *1.LC*
*__smoke__ [sməʊk] rauchen 6.8
smoking ['sməʊkɪŋ] Raucher(abteil) 4.8
smuggle ['smʌgl] schmuggeln *7.5*
snack [snæk] Snack, Imbiss *3.LC*
sneeze [sniːz] niesen 12.S3
snow [snəʊ] Schnee *H3*
snow [snəʊ] schneien 1.S1
so [səʊ] so, in dieser Weise; deshalb, daher, also 1.1
social ['səʊʃl] sozial, gesellschaftlich, gesellig *1.LC*, 11.S1
society [sə'saɪətɪ] Gesellschaft 10.S1
*__some__ [sʌm] einige, manche, etwas 1.I
*__someone__ ['sʌmwʌn] (irgend)jemand 1.9
*__something__ ['sʌmθɪŋ] (irgend)etwas 4.S4
sometimes ['sʌmtaɪmz] manchmal 7.7
somewhere ['sʌmweə] irgendwo(hin) 2.S5: **somewhere else** irgendwo anders *6.LC*
*__son__ [sʌn] Sohn 3.S4
song [sɒŋ] Lied *H1*
*__soon__ [suːn] bald H3
*__sorry__ ['sɒrɪ]: **(I'm) sorry** es tut mir Leid 2.S7
*__sort__ [sɔːt] Sorte, Art 3.S5
sound [saʊnd] Klang, Ton, Geräusch *9.I*
sound [saʊnd] klingen, sich anhören 6.2
*__soup of the day__ [ˌsuːp‿əv ðə 'deɪ] Tagessuppe 6.2
*__south__ [saʊθ] Süden, Süd- H2: **South African** Südafrikaner/in; südafrikanisch *H2*
souvenir [ˌsuːvə'nɪə] Souvenir, Andenken 4.2
soya sauce ['sɔɪə sɔːs] Sojasauce *H3*
space [speɪs] Platz, Lücke, Raum *1.9*
*__speak__ [spiːk] sprechen 1.S6
special ['speʃl] Sonderangebot 8.2
special ['speʃl] besondere(r, s) *2.5*, 4.8
speciality [ˌspeʃɪ'ælətɪ] Spezialität 3.10
species ['spiːʃiːz] Spezies, Art, Gattung *H1*
spectacular [spek'tækjʊlə] spektakulär 8.S1
speculator ['spekjʊleɪtə] Spekulant/in, Investor/in *H2*
speed [spiːd] Geschwindigkeit *8.TT*: **speed limit** Geschwindigkeitsbegrenzung *8.TT*
*__spell__ [spel] buchstabieren 8.2
spend [spend] *hier:* verbringen *1.I*, 9.S1
*__spend (money)__ [spend ('mʌnɪ)] (Geld) ausgeben 7.4
spicy ['spaɪsɪ] würzig, scharf 6.3
spirit ['spɪrɪt] Geist *10.S1*
splendid ['splendɪd] wunderschön, herrlich *10.S1*
split up [splɪt‿'ʌp] aufteilen *4.9*
spontaneous [spɒn'teɪnɪəs] spontan *6.4*
*__sports__ [spɔːts] Sport 2.8: **sports car** Sportwagen 7.2: **sports plane** Sportflugzeug 7.S5
sportsman ['spɔːtsmən] Sportler, Athlet *H3*
spot [spɒt] finden, ausfindig machen, erkennen *12.5*
spotlight ['spɒtlaɪt] Scheinwerfer, Spot *H1*
spring [sprɪŋ] Frühling 6.7
springbok ['sprɪŋbɒk] Springbock *H2*
square [skweə] Quadrat, Kästchen *10.7*: **square (kilo)metre** Quadrat(kilo)meter 11.6; **square dance** *amerik. Volkstanz H1*
stadium ['steɪdjəm] Stadion 11.S5
staff [stɑːf] Mitarbeiter *(Mz)* 9.4
stall-holder ['stɔːlˌhəʊldə] Standbetreiber/in, Händler/in *10.5*
*__stamp__ [stæmp] Briefmarke 8.S5
*__stand__ [stænd] stehen 12.2: **stand in line** anstehen, Schlange stehen *H1*
standard ['stændəd] Standard *5.LC*
star [stɑː] Stern *H1*
start [stɑːt] Anfang, Beginn *H2*
*__start__ [stɑːt] anfangen, beginnen 2.3
starter [ˌstɑːtə] Einstieg 1.1
*__starter__ ['stɑːtə] *hier:* Vorspeise 6.2
state [steɪt] (Bundes)Staat 2.S1
station ['steɪʃn] Station *H2*: **service station** Tankstelle *IP.1*
*__station__ ['steɪʃn] Bahnhof 2.S5
statistics *(Mz)* [stə'tɪstɪks] Statistik *7.4*
statue ['stætʃuː] Statue 7.2
status ['steɪtəs] Status *8.4*
stay [steɪ] Aufenthalt 12.2
*__stay__ [steɪ] bleiben, sich aufhalten 1.I
*__steak__ [steɪk] Steak 6.2
steal [stiːl] stehlen 7.5
*__steel__ [stiːl] Stahl 10.S1
steering [stiːrɪŋ] Lenkung *IP.1*
sticker ['stɪkə] Aufkleber *8.1*
still [stɪl] (immer) noch *1.TT*
*__stop__ [stɒp] anhalten, stoppen, aufhören 4.S1: **stop off** Zwischenstation machen *9.I*
store [stɔː] speichern, unterbringen 10.2
storm [stɔːm] Sturm 6.S1
*__story__ ['stɔːrɪ] Geschichte, Erzählung 4.2
straight [streɪt] gerade 10.S1: **straight on** geradeaus *9.8*
strap [stræp] Gurt, Träger *5.2*
*__street__ [striːt] Straße H1
strict [strɪkt] streng *12.TT*
stripe [straɪp] Streifen *H1*
strong [strɒŋ] stark 6.S1
*__student__ ['stjuːdənt] Student/in, Kursteilnehmer/in 1.8
style [staɪl] Stil 9.2
submarine ['sʌbməriːn] U-Boot *H1*
such [sʌtʃ] so, solch *H3*
suffer (from) ['sʌfə (frəm)] leiden (an/unter) 7.2
sugar ['ʃʊgə] Zucker *H2*
suggest [sə'dʒest] vorschlagen *2.7*
suggestion [sə'dʒestʃən] Vorschlag *2.7*
suitcase ['suːtkeɪs] Koffer 5.2
summer ['sʌmə] Sommer 1.I
sun [sʌn] Sonne 6.S1: **sun block** Sonnencreme 6.2; **sun cream** Sonnencreme 10.1
sunbathe ['sʌnbeɪð] sonnen, sonnenbaden 7.9
sunburn ['sʌnbɜːn] Sonnenbrand *IP.2*
Sunday ['sʌndɪ] Sonntag 2.7: **on Sundays** sonntags 2.S7
sunglasses *(Mz)* ['sʌnglɑːsɪz] Sonnenbrille 5.4
*__sunny__ ['sʌnɪ] sonnig 6.S2
sunshine ['sʌnʃaɪn] Sonnenschein 6.2
sunstroke ['sʌnstrəʊk] Sonnenstich, Hitzeschlag 8.S1
superb [sʊ'pɜːb] hervorragend, ausgezeichnet *H2*
superlative [suː'pɜːlətɪv] Superlativ, 2. Steigerungsform *3.5*
suppose [sə'pəʊz] annehmen, vermuten 8.2
*__sure__ [ʃɔː] sicher 1.S1: **make sure** sichergehen, sich vergewissern *5.TT*, 11.S1
surname ['sɜːneɪm] Nachname, Familienname 8.4

surprised [sə'praɪzd] überrascht, verwundert *4.LC*
survive [sə'vaɪv] überleben, überstehen *H2*
swim [swɪm]: **go for a swim** schwimmen gehen 7.8
* **swim** [swɪm] schwimmen 7.S4
swimming pool ['swɪmɪŋ ˌpuːl] Schwimmbad, -becken 4.S3
Swiss [swɪs] schweizerische(r, s); Schweizer/in *11.TT*
switch on [swɪtʃ‿'ɒn] an-/einschalten 10.2
symbol ['sɪmbl] Symbol, (Wahr)Zeichen *7.7*, 10.2
symptom ['sɪmptəm] (Krankheits-) Symptom *IP.2*
system ['sɪstəm] System *1.TT*

T

t-shirt ['tiːʃɜːt] T-Shirt 10.6
table ['teɪbl] *hier:* Tabelle *1.TT*; Tisch 3.10
tablet ['tæblɪt] Tablette *IP.2*
* **take** [teɪk] (mit)nehmen 1.7
take [teɪk] *hier:* brauchen, dauern 4.8: **take off** starten, abheben *(Flugzeug)* 7.S4; *hier:* ausziehen *11.LC*; **take photos** fotografieren 4.2; **take turns** sich abwechseln *2.5*
take off ['teɪk‿ɒf] Start *(Flug)* 12.2
tale [teɪl] Geschichte, Erzählung 4.2
* **talk** [tɔːk] reden 1.S6
tall [tɔːl] groß 7.2
taste [teɪst] schmecken, probieren 3.2
* **tax** [tæks] Steuer 11.S1
* **taxi** ['tæksɪ] Taxi 1.2
* **tea** [tiː] Tee 6.8
teacher ['tiːtʃə] Lehrer/in, Kursleiter/in *2.8*, 4.S4
teaching ['tiːtʃɪŋ] Lehre 9.S1
team [tiːm] Gruppe, Mannschaft, Team *2.8*
tear [tɪə] Träne *H3*
* **telephone** ['telɪfəʊn] Telefon 6.S5
telephone ['telɪfəʊn] anrufen, telefonieren 5.2
* **television (TV)** ['telɪˌvɪʒn (tiː'viː)] Fernsehen, Fernseher 10.S5
* **tell** [tel] erzählen, sagen 1.5
temperature ['temprətʃə] Temperatur 6.S1
* **temperature** ['temprətʃə] erhöhte Temperatur *IP.2*
temple ['templ] Tempel *11.LC*
tense [tens] Zeit *(gramm.) 7.S5*
term [tɜːm] Zeit, Dauer *H2*
* **terrible** ['terəbl] schrecklich 5.8
territory ['terɪtɒrɪ] (Hoheits-, Staats) Gebiet *9.S1*, 11.S1
* **test** [test] Test, Prüfung 7.2
text [tekst] Text *1.3*
* **than** [ðæn] als *(Vergleich)* 3.S2
* **thank you** ['θæŋk juː] danke 1.S1
thanks [θæŋks] danke 1.2
* **that** [ðæt] das (dort) 2.2
* **the** [ðə, ðɪ] der, die, das 1.l
* **theatre** ['θɪətə] Theater 2.8
* **their** [ðeə] ihr/e *(Mz)* 1.l
theirs [ðeəz] ihre(r,s) 5.2
* **them** [ðem, ðəm] sie, ihnen *(Mz)* 1.l
theme [θiːm] Thema, Motto 9.S1: **theme park** Freizeitpark 9.S1
* **themselves** [ðəm'selvz] sie *(Mz)* sich selbst 4.6
* **then** [ðen] *hier:* da, damals 8.S1; dann 1.1
theory ['θɪərɪ] Theorie 2.2
* **there** [ðeə] dort 1.2: * **over there** da/dort drüben 1.7; **there is/are** es gibt 1.7
* **these** [ðiːz] diese *(Mz)* 1.2
* **they** [ðeɪ] sie *(Mz)* 1.l
thick [θɪk] dick *H2*
* **thing** [θɪŋ] Ding, Sache 1.9
* **think** [θɪŋk] denken, glauben, meinen 1.TT: **think about** nachdenken über 10.S6; **think of** denken an, sich ausdenken *6.1*, 6.S1; **I think so** ich glaube schon 6.2
* **this** [ðɪs] diese(r, s) 1.1
thousands ['θaʊzəndz] Tausende *H1*
through [θruː] durch 10.S1
thunder ['θʌndə] Donner 6.S1
Thursday ['θɜːzdeɪ] Donnerstag 2.7
tick [tɪk] Haken, Häkchen *7.5*
tick [tɪk] ankreuzen, abhaken *1.6*
* **ticket** ['tɪkɪt] Eintritts-, Fahrkarte, Ticket 3.S8
* **time** [taɪm] Zeit 1.7: **in time** rechtzeitig 4.S1; **on time** pünktlich 12.2; **this time** dieses Mal 3.7; **time zone** Zeitzone *2.TT*; * **what time?** (um) wie viel Uhr? 2.9
* **times** [taɪmz]: **... times** ...mal H2
tiny ['taɪnɪ] winzig 11.S1
tip [tɪp] Tipp, Hinweis *1.TT*
* **tip** [tɪp] Trinkgeld 7.S4
tip [tɪp] Trinkgeld geben *6.TT*
* **tired** ['taɪəd] müde E.2
* **to** [tʊ, tə] zu, mit, nach 1.l; vor (Uhrzeit) 2.S3
* **today** [tʊ'deɪ] heute 2.S1
* **together** [tə'geðə] zusammen 3.S5
toilet ['tɔɪlɪt] Toilette *7.LC*
toll [təʊl] Gebühr, Maut *8.TT*
tomato (tomatoes) [tə'mɑːtəʊ (tə'mɑːtəʊz)] Tomate 6.3
* **tomorrow** [tə'mɒrəʊ] morgen 2.S7
tone [təʊn] Ton 5.S1
tonic ['tɒnɪk] Tonic 3.7
* **too** [tuː] auch *(nachgestellt)* 2.S5; (all)zu 4.8
* **tooth (teeth)** [tuːθ (tiːθ)] Zahn 8.6
* **top** [tɒp] Spitze 7.2
* **top** [tɒp] Ober-, oberste(r, s) 7.2
topless ['tɒpləs] ohne Oberteil, oben ohne *11.LC*
tough [tʌf] streng, hart 8.S1
* **tour** [tʊə] Tour, Ausflug, Reise 2.9: **tour guide** Reiseführer/in, -leiter/in *H2*
* **tourist** ['tʊərɪst] Tourist/in 1.l: **tourist board** Fremdenverkehrsamt 11.S1; **tourist information centre** Fremdenverkehrsbüro, Touristeninformation 8.8
tower ['taʊə] Turm 10.S1
* **town** [taʊn] Stadt 2.8
trading ['treɪdɪŋ] Handel, Handels- *H2*
traditional [trə'dɪʃənl] traditionell, herkömmlich 10.S1
traffic-lights ['træfɪklaɪts] Verkehrsampel *H2*
* **train** [treɪn] Zug 2.S3
trainer ['treɪnə] Trainer/in *H3*
transport ['trænspɔːt] Transport 1.7: **public transport** öffentliche Verkehrsmittel 3.4
* **travel** ['trævl] reisen 1.1: **travel agent** Reisekaufmann, -frau *9.TT*; **travel sickness** Reisekrankheit *IP.2*
tree [triː] Baum *5.6*
trekking ['trekɪŋ] Wandern *H2*
trend [trend] Trend, Bewegung, Richtung *H2*
tribal ['traɪbl] Stammes- *H2*
trick [trɪk]: **play a trick** Streich spielen *12.S1*
* **trip** [trɪp] Reise, Ausflug 2.2
trolley ['trɒlɪ] Gepäckwagen 1.2
tropical ['trɒpɪkl] tropisch 6.S1
* **trousers** *(Mz)* ['traʊzəz] Hosen 5.4
truck *(AE)* [trʌk] Lieferwagen, Lastwagen *8.5*
* **true** [truː] wahr 1.7
try (out) [traɪ (aʊt)] versuchen, (aus)probieren 3.7: **try on** anprobieren 10.5
Tuesday ['tjuːzdeɪ] Dienstag 2.2
turn [tɜːn]: **my turn** ich bin dran/an der Reihe 6.2; **take turns** sich abwechseln *2.5*; **in turns** abwechselnd *2.7*
turn [tɜːn] *hier:* blättern *2.8*; wenden, abbiegen 9.8
tusk [tʌsk] Stoßzahn *H2*
twice [twaɪs] zweimal *3.S4*, 8.7
type [taɪp] Typ, Art, Sorte 5.S1
typical ['tɪpɪkl] typisch 1.S1

U

ugly ['ʌglɪ] hässlich 3.5
unattended [ˌʌnə'tendɪd] unbeaufsichtigt 12.2
uncomfortable [ʌn'kʌmfətæbl] unbequem 3.5
uncomplicated [ʌn'kɒmplɪkeɪtɪd] unkompliziert *H1*
uncountable [ˌʌn'kaʊntəbl] nicht zählbar *10.6*
* **under** ['ʌndə] unter 3.LC
underline [ˌʌndə'laɪn] unterstreichen *1.4*
underneath [ˌʌndə'niːθ] unterhalb, darunter *8.1*
* **understand** [ˌʌndə'stænd] verstehen 4.LC
underwater [ˌʌndə'wɔːtə] Unterwasser- *H2*
unforgettable [ˌʌnfə'getəbl] unvergesslich *H2*
unhappy [ʌn'hæpɪ] unglücklich 11.S1
uniform ['juːnɪfɔːm] Uniform *9.LC*
unit ['juːnɪt] Lektion, Kapitel; Einheit *6.8*

united [jʊ'naɪtɪd] vereinigt *H1*
* **university** [ˌjuːnɪ'vɜːsətɪ] Universität 2.8
unlimited [ʌn'lɪmɪtɪd] unbegrenzt, uneingeschränkt 8.2
unlucky [ʌn'lʌkɪ] Unglücks-, Pech- *10.LC*
* **until** [ʌn'tɪl] bis H1
unused [ʌn'juːzd] unbenutzt *5.S1*
unusual [ʌn'juːʒʊəl] ungewöhnlich *5.I*, 10.S1
* **up** [ʌp] hoch, oben auf 6.2
up-to-date [ˌʌptə'deɪt] aktuell *11.TT*
* **us** [ʌs] uns 10.2
use [juːs] Gebrauch, Nutzen, Benutzung 8.2
* **use** [juːz] benutzen, gebrauchen 1.7
useful ['juːsfʊl] nützlich *3.TT*
* **usually** ['juːʒəlɪ] normalerweise, gewöhnlich 4.TT

V

vacate [və'keɪt] frei machen, räumen *9.6*
vacation *(AE)* [və'keɪʃn] Ferien, Urlaub *H1*
vaccination [ˌvæksɪ'neɪʃn] Impfung *9.TT*: **certificate of vaccination** Impfpass *9.TT*
valid ['vælɪd] gültig *8.TT*
valley ['vælɪ] Tal *11.S1*
value ['væljuː] Wert 5.S1
variety [və'raɪətɪ] Vielfalt *H1*
vast [vɑːst] riesig, weit *H1*
* **vegetable(s)** ['vedʒtəbl(z)] Gemüse 6.2
vegetation [ˌvedʒɪ'teɪʃn] Vegetation, Pflanzen *H2*
vehicle ['viːɪkl] Fahrzeug 8.2
verb [vɜːb] Verb, Zeitwort *4.1*
vertically ['vɜːtɪklɪ] vertikal, senkrecht *10.7*
* **very** ['verɪ] sehr 1.3
* **view (of)** [vjuː (ɒv)] Aussicht (auf) 6.2
* **village** ['vɪlɪdʒ] Dorf 4.2
visa ['viːzə] Visum *11.TT*
* **visit** ['vɪzɪt] Besuch 2.S1
* **visit** ['vɪzɪt] besuchen 2.6
visitor ['vɪzɪtə] Besucher/in 2.S7

W

* **wait (for)** [weɪt (fə)] warten (auf) 5.9
* **waiter, waitress** ['weɪtə, 'weɪtrɪs] Kellner/in 5.S8
walk [wɔːk] Spaziergang 2.9
* **walk** [wɔːk] (zu Fuß) gehen 1.9
wall [wɔːl] Wand, Mauer 4.2
walnut ['wɔːlnʌt] Walnuss 6.3
* **want** [wɒnt] wollen 1.1
wardrobe ['wɔːdrəʊb] Garderobe, Schrank *9.7*
* **warm** [wɔːm] warm 2.S5
warn [wɔːn] warnen *H2*
* **wash** [wɒʃ] (sich) waschen 9.7
* **watch** [wɒtʃ] (Armband)Uhr 5.S3
watch [wɒtʃ] zuschauen *H3*
* **water** ['wɔːtə] Wasser 7-9
waterfall ['wɔːtəfɔːl] Wasserfall *4.3*
waters *(Mz)* ['wɔːtəz] Gewässer *H2*
way [weɪ] Art, Weise *1.3*, 8.2
* **we** [wiː] wir 1.2
wealth [welθ] Reichtum *H2*
wealthy ['welθɪ] reich, wohlhabend *H1*
wear [weə] tragen *(Kleidung)* 1.S1
* **weather** ['weðə] Wetter 3.4
website ['websaɪt] Internetseite 8.2
wedding ['wedɪŋ] Hochzeit, Heirat 4.S1
* **Wednesday** ['wenzdeɪ] Mittwoch 2.7
* **week** [wiːk] Woche 1.I
* **weekend** [ˌwiːk'end] Wochenende 1.9
weigh [weɪ] wiegen *H2*
weight [weɪt] Gewicht 9.6
welcome ['welkəm] willkommen heißen *1.I*: * **you're welcome** bitte sehr, gern geschehen E.1; * **welcome (to)** willkommen (in/bei) 1.2
* **well** [wel] gut 1.3
well [wel] nun, tja, nun ja 1.2
well-known ['welnəʊn] wohlbekannt *H3*
well-paid [wel'peɪd] gut bezahlt *H2*
well-watered [wel'wɔːtəd] gut bewässert *H3*
Welshman ['welʃmən] Waliser *H3*
were [wɜː] *hier:* wäre *(Konjunktiv)* *11.1*
Western ['westən] westlich *10.LC*
* **wet** [wet] nass *9.7*
whale [weɪl] Wal *H2*
* **what** [wɒt] was 1.2: * **What about ...?** Wie ist es mit ...? 2.S7; * **what time?** (um) wie viel Uhr? 5.8; **What's on?** Was läuft? Was steht auf dem Programm? *2.1*; **What's wrong?** Was stimmt nicht? Was ist los? Was ist passiert? *2.S3*
wheel [wiːl] Rad *H3*
* **when** [wen] wenn, wann 1.9; als 2.S7
* **where** [weə] wo(hin, -her) 1.2
whether ['weðə] ob 10.2
* **which** [wɪtʃ] welche(r, s) 1.3
whisky ['wɪskɪ] Whisky 1.S1
* **white** [waɪt] weiß 5.S4
who [huː] *hier:* der, die, das *(Relativpronomen) 1.9*
* **who** [huː] wer, wem, wen 3.8
whole [həʊl] ganz 12.S1
whose [huːz] wessen 5.3
* **why** [waɪ] warum 2.2
* **wide** [waɪd] breit 8.S1
* **wife (wives)** [waɪf (waɪvz)] Ehefrau 5.S6
wild [waɪld] wild *H2*
wildlife ['waɪldlaɪf] Natur, Wildnis, Tier- und Pflanzenwelt *H1*
* **will** [wɪl] werden *(Zukunft)* 1.TT
win [wɪn] gewinnen, siegen 11.S1
wind [wɪnd] Wind 6.S1
* **window** ['wɪndəʊ] Fenster 6.2
* **windy** ['wɪndɪ] windig 6.7
* **wine** [waɪn] Wein 6.2: **table wine** Tafel-, Tischwein 4.3
winner ['wɪnə] Gewinner/in, Sieger/in *11.5*
* **winter** ['wɪntə] Winter 1.S1
wish [wɪʃ] (sich) wünschen *11.1*
* **with** [wɪð] mit 1.7
withdraw [wɪð'drɔː] abheben 10.2
* **woman (women)** ['wʊmən ('wɪmɪn)] Frau 4.S1
won't (= will not) [wəʊnt] *Verneinung von will* 6.6
wonder ['wʌndə] Wunder *H1*
wonderful ['wʌndəfʊl] wunderbar 1.2
wooden ['wʊdn] hölzern, Holz- 9.S1
* **word** [wɜːd] Wort 1.3
wordsearch ['wɜːdsɜːtʃ] Wortsuche *10.7*
* **work** [wɜːk] Arbeit 1.7: **at work** in/bei der Arbeit 1.6
* **work** [wɜːk] arbeiten 1.7: **work (out)** *hier:* funktionieren *H3*, 10.2; **work out** herausarbeiten, herausfinden *12.6*
worker ['wɜːkə] Arbeiter/in *H2*
* **world** [wɜːld] Welt 2.S1
worry ['wʌrɪ] Sorge, Besorgnis *5.LC*, 6.2: **Don't worry!** Mach dir / Machen Sie sich / Macht euch keine Sorgen! 5.2
worse [wɜːs] schlechter, schlimmer 3.S7
worst [wɜːst]: **the worst** am schlechtesten/schlimmsten 3.6
* **would** [wʊd] würde(st/n/t) 2.S7: * **I would like (= I'd)** ich möchte/hätte gerne 2.S7
wrap [ræp] einwickeln, einpacken 12.9
* **write** [raɪt] schreiben 10.S4: **write (down)** (auf)schreiben *1.9*
* **wrong** [rɒŋ] falsch 2.S3

Y

yacht [jɒt] Yacht *2.S1*
yard [jɑːd] Yard *(Längenmaß) 1.TT*
* **year** [jɪə] Jahr 1.S6
year-round [jɪə'raʊnd] ganzjährig *H3*
* **yellow** ['jeləʊ] gelb 5.8: **yellow fever** Gelbfieber *9.TT*
* **yes** [jes] ja 1.2
* **yesterday** ['jestədeɪ] gestern 10.S5
* **yet** [jet] schon, bereits 6.2: **not yet** noch nicht 8.S5
yet [jet] *hier:* trotzdem, dennoch *H1*
* **you** [juː] du, dich, dir; Sie, Ihnen; ihr, euch 1.1
* **young** [jʌŋ] jung 12.S1
* **your** [jɔː] Ihr/e, dein/e, euer/eure 1.1
yours [jɔːz] deine(r,s), Ihre(r,s), eure(r,s) 5.S2
* **yourself** [jɔː'self] du dir/dich selbst, Sie sich selbst 1.1

Z

zebra ['zebrə] Zebra *H2*
zone [zəʊn] Zone *2.TT*

PEOPLE AND PLACES

Names

Girls/Women

Katy ['keɪtɪ]
Liz [lɪz]
Mary ['meərɪ]
Padma ['pædmə]
Pam [pæm]
Sarah ['seərə]

Boys/Men

Andrew ['ændruː]
Francis ['frɑːnsɪs]
James [dʒeɪmz]
Jay [dʒeɪ]
Joe [dʒəʊ]
Paul [pɔːl]
Peter ['piːtə]
Sam [sæm]
Simon ['saɪmən]
Steven ['stiːvn]
Thomas ['tɒməs]

Families

Grainger ['greɪndʒə]
Lerner ['lɜːnə]
Lowe [ləʊ]

Other Names

42nd Street [ˌfɔːtɪ'sekənd striːt]
Abraham Lincoln [ˌeɪbrəm 'lɪnkən]
Afrikaans [ˌæfrɪ'kɑːns]
Al Capone [æl kə'pəʊn]
Algonquin [æl'gɒnkwɪn]
Anangu [ə'næŋgʊ]
ANC (= African National Congress) [eɪensiː (ˌæfrɪkən‿ˌnæʃənl 'kɒŋgres)]
Antelope Canyon [ˌæntɪləʊp 'kænjən]
Anton Rupert [ˌæntɒn 'ruːpət]
Australia Day [ɒ'streɪlɪə ˌdeɪ]
Bantu ['bʌntʊ]
Bingo ['bɪŋgəʊ]
Bird Paradise [ˌbɜːd 'pærədaɪz]
Bloomingdale's ['bluːmɪŋdeɪlz]
Bob Furguson [ˌbɒb 'fɜːgəsn]
Braid Hills [breɪd 'hɪlz]
Britannia [brɪ'tænɪə]
Bryce Canyon [braɪs 'kænjən]
Camelot ['kæməlɒt]
Canada Day ['kænədə ˌdeɪ]
Cantonese [ˌkæntə'niːz]
Cats [kæts]
Celsius ['selsjəs]
Central Park [ˌsentrəl 'pɑːk]
Christmas Day [ˌkrɪsməs 'deɪ]
Citic Tower ['sɪtɪk taʊə]
Columbus [kə'lʌmbəs]
Commonwealth ['kɒmənwelθ]
Daihatsu Charade [daɪ'hætsuː ʃə'rɑːd]
David Niven [ˌdeɪvɪd 'nɪvən]
Deacon Brown [ˌdiːkən 'braʊn]
Death Valley [deθ 'vælɪ]
Down Under [daʊn‿'ʌndə]
Edinburgh Castle [ˌedɪnbrə 'kɑːsl]
Eleanor Roosevelt [ˌelɪənɔː 'rəʊzvelt]
Ernest Gosse [ˌɜːnəst 'gɒs]
Errol Flynn [ˌerəl 'flɪn]
Fahrenheit ['færənhaɪt]
Fifth Avenue [fɪfθ‿'ævənjuː]
Film Fantasia ['fɪlm fænˌteɪʒə]
Fisherman's Wharf [ˌfɪʃəmənz 'wɔːf]
Frank Lloyd Wright [ˌfræŋk ˌlɔɪd 'raɪt]
Freedom Day ['friːdəm ˌdeɪ]
George Washington [ˌdʒɔːdʒ 'wɒʃɪŋtən]
Glasgow Central [ˌglɑːzgəʊ 'sentrəl]
Golden Gate Bridge [ˌgəʊldən geɪt 'brɪdʒ]
Goldfish Garden [ˌgəʊldfɪʃ 'gɑːdn]
Grauman's Chinese Theatre [ˌgraʊmənz tʃaɪˌniːz 'θɪətə]
Guinness ['gɪnɪs]
haggis ['hægɪs]
Hammacher Schlemmer [ˌhæmækə 'ʃlemə]
Hard Rock Café ['hɑːd rɒk‿kæˌfeɪ]
Harley Davidson [ˌhɑːlɪ 'deɪvɪdzn]
Hindi ['hɪndiː]
Independence Day [ˌɪndɪ'pendəns ˌdeɪ]
J. F. Kennedy [ˌdʒeɪ‿ef 'kenədɪ]
Jumbo Restaurant [ˌdʒʌmbəʊ 'restərɑːnt]
Kids' World ['kɪdz wɜːld]
Kingsford Smith [ˌkɪŋzfəd 'smɪθ]
Kowloon [kaʊ'luːn]
Lantau [læn'taʊ]
Lei Garden [leɪ 'gɑːdn]
Li Yuen [ˌliː jʊ'en]
Macy's ['meɪsɪz]
Maori ['maʊrɪ]
Marble Dry-Goods Palace [ˌmɑːbl ˌdraɪgʊdz 'pæləs]
Marilyn Monroe [ˌmeərəlɪn mɒn'rəʊ]
Metropolitan Opera [metrəʊˌpɒlɪtn‿'ɒprə]
Mount Rushmore National Memorial [maʊnt ˌrʌʃmɔː ˌnæʃənl mə'mɔːrɪəl]
Native American [ˌneɪtɪv‿ə'merɪkən]
Natural Museum [ˌnætʃərəl mjuː'ziːəm]
Nobel Peace Prize [nəʊˌbəl 'piːs praɪz]
Ocean Park ['əʊʃn pɑːk]
Patois ['pʌtwɑː]
Peak Tram [piːk 'træm]
Plaza Hotel ['plɑːzə ˌhəʊ'tel]
Prime Minister [praɪm 'mɪnɪstə]
Princes Street ['prɪnsɪz ˌstriːt]
Protea [prəʊ'tiːə]
Qantas ['kwɒntəs]
Rastafarian [ˌræstə'færɪən]
Red Stripe [red 'straɪp]
Regent Hotel [ˌriːdʒənt həʊ'tel]
Royal Mile [ˌrɔɪəl 'maɪl]
Saint Giles [sənt 'gaɪlz]
Saint Mary [sənt 'meərɪ]
Saks [sæks]
Samsonite ['sæmsənaɪt]
San [sɑːn]
Shakespeare ['ʃeɪkspɪə]
Sir Henry Ayers [sɜː ˌhenrɪ‿'eəz]
Sir Henry Morgan [sɜː ˌhenrɪ 'mɔːgən]
St Andrew's Day [snt‿'ændruːz ˌdeɪ]
St David's Day [snt 'deɪvɪdz ˌdeɪ]
St George's Day [snt 'dʒɔːdʒəz ˌdeɪ]
St Patrick's Day [snt 'pætrɪks ˌdeɪ]
Stanley Market [ˌstænlɪ 'mɑːkɪt]
Star Ferry ['stɑː ferɪ]
Statue of Liberty [ˌstætjuː‿əv 'lɪbətɪ]
Sydney Harbour Bridge [sɪdnɪ ˌhɑːbə 'brɪdʒ]
Taino ['taɪnəʊ]
Telstra ['telstrə]
Theodore Roosevelt [ˌθɪədɔː 'rəʊzvelt]
Thomas Jefferson [ˌtɒməs 'dʒefəsən]
Time out ['taɪm‿aʊt]
Transfrontier Peace Park [trænsfrɒn'tɪə 'piːs pɑːk]
Tsing Ma Bridge [tsɪŋ ˌmɑː 'brɪdʒ]
Victoria Harbour [vɪkˌtɒrɪə 'hɑːbə]
Victoria Peak [vɪkˌtɒrɪə 'piːk]
Village Voice [ˌvɪlɪdʒ 'vɔɪs]
Waldorf Astoria [ˌwɔːldɔːf‿ə'stɔːrɪə]
Waverley ['weɪvəlɪ]
Willie Park Junior [ˌwɪlɪ pɑːk 'dʒuːnjə]
Winston Watt [ˌwɪnstən 'wɒt]
Yosemite Natinal Park [jəʊˌsemɪtɪ næʃənl 'pɑːk]

Place Names

Aberdeen [ˌæbə'diːn]
Africa ['æfrɪkə]
The Alps [ðɪ‿'ælps]
America [ə'merɪkə]
Asia ['eɪʃə]
Australia [ɒ'streɪlɪə]
Austria ['ɔːstrɪə]
Ayers Rock [ˌeəz 'rɒk]
Bangkok ['bæŋkɒk]
Barbados [bɑː'beɪdɒs]
Ben Nevis [ben‿'nevɪs]
Blackhead Mountains [ˌblækhed 'maʊntɪnz]
Blue Mountains [bluː 'maʊntɪnz]
Bondi Beach [ˌbɒndɪ 'biːtʃ]
Bradford ['brædfəd]
Britain ['brɪtn]
California [ˌkælə'fɔːnɪə]
Canada ['kænədə]
Cape Town ['keɪp taʊn]
China ['tʃaɪnə]
Cockpit Country [ˌkɒkpɪt 'kʌntrɪ]
Drakensberg Mountains [ˌdreɪkənsbɜːg 'maʊntɪnz]
Drumnadrochit [ˌdrʌmnə'drɒkɪt]
Durban ['dɜːbən]
Edinburgh ['edɪnbrə]
Egypt ['iːdʒɪpt]
England ['ɪŋglənd]
Ethiopia [ˌiːθɪ'əʊpɪə]
Europe ['jʊərəp]
Germany ['dʒɜːmənɪ]
Glenfellet [glen'felət]
Gretna Green [ˌgretnə 'griːn]
Heathrow [ˌhiːθ'rəʊ]
Highgate ['haɪgeɪt]
Highland ['haɪlənd]
India ['ɪndɪə]
Inverness [ˌɪnvə'nes]
Ireland ['aɪələnd]
Italy ['ɪtəlɪ]
Jamaica [dʒə'meɪkə]
Japan [dʒə'pæn]
Johannesburg [dʒəʊ'hænəsbɜːg]
Kenya ['kenjə]
Kimberley ['kɪmbəlɪ]
Kingston ['kɪŋstən]
Kruger National Park ['kruːgə ˌnæʃənəl ˌpɑːk]
Las Vegas [læs 'veɪgəs]
Liberty Island [ˌlɪbətɪ‿'aɪlənd]
Limpopo [lɪm'pəʊpəʊ]
Loch Lomond [lɒk 'ləʊmənd]
Loch Ness [lɒk 'nes]
London ['lʌndən]
Montego Bay [mɒnˌtiːgəʊ 'beɪ]
Moravia [mə'reɪvɪə]
Mozambique [ˌməʊzæm'biːk]
Munich ['mjuːnɪk]
Musselburgh ['mʌslbrə]
The Netherlands [ðə 'neðələndz]
Niagara Falls [naɪˌægərə 'fɔːlz]
Oudtshoorn ['aʊtshɔːn]
Pacific [pə'sɪfɪk]
Parramatta [ˌpærə'mætə]
Pennsylvania [ˌpensl'veɪnɪə]
Port Elizabeth [ˌpɔːt‿ə'lɪzəbeθ]
Portugal ['pɔːtʃʊgl]
Pretoria [prɪ'tɔːrɪə]
Queensland ['kwiːnzlənd]
Robben Island [ˌrɒbən‿'aɪlənd]
San Francisco [ˌsæn frən'sɪskəʊ]
Scotland ['skɒtlənd]
Scottish Islands [ˌskɒtɪʃ‿'aɪləndz]
Seaford Town [ˌsiːfəd 'taʊn]
Sha Tin [ʃɑː 'tɪn]
South Africa [ˌsaʊθ‿'æfrɪkə]
Soweto [səʊ'wiːtəʊ]
Spain [speɪn]
St Barthelemy [sənt bɑː'θeləmɪ]
Table Mountain [ˌteɪbl 'maʊntɪn]
Thailand ['taɪlænd]
UK (United Kingdom) [ˌjuː'keɪ (jʊˌnaɪtɪd 'kɪŋdəm)]
Uluru [ʊ'luːrʊ]
USA [ˌjuː es 'eɪ]
Wales [weɪlz]
West Indies [west‿'ɪndɪz]
Western Australia [ˌwestən‿ɒ'streɪlɪə]
Xiang Gang [ksɪæŋ 'gæŋ]
Zimbabwe [zɪm'bʌbwɪ]
Zurich ['zʊərɪk]

Acknowledgement

The material reproduced in this book has been taken from the following sources:

Illustrations
Jürgen Bartz, München: page 4, 5, 6, 19, 39 (left), 42, 47, 48, 54, 55, 57 (middle), 59, 69 (bottom), 70, 77 (top), 79 (top), 80 – Fran Jordan, Ilkley: page 35, 37, 41, 43, 57 (top), 65, 69 (top), 77 (bottom), 79 (bottom) – Graham Round (Linda Rogers Associates), London: page 30, 52, 74 – Dave Vaughan, München: page 75

Photographs
Beate Andler-Teufel, München: page 28 (top), 28 , 29, 36 (top right), 46 (2nd from bottom), 63 (right), 66 (top right) – Auckland Tourism: page 40 (top right) – Axiom Photographic Agency Ltd., London: page 73 (bottom) – BAA Aviation Picture Library: page 10 (background) – Colin Baxter: page 7 (top), 14 (top right), 9 (background) – Christiane Bohner, München: page 13 (bottom) – BridgeClimb Sydney: page 40 (bottom) – Graham Brownbill, Salisbury: page 16 (bottom), 21 – www.britainonview.com: page 11 (3), 17 (top right), 20 (left), 24 (bottom) – CINETEXT: page 72 (middle right) – Corbis GmbH, Düsseldorf: page cover (insert), 3 (bottom), 8 (2nd from bottom), 9 (bottom), 10 (top left), 12 (top), 16 (top), 26 (bottom right) (bottom left), 27 (top right), 31 (bottom), 46 (bottom), 49 (bottom), 53 (left), 54 (middle left) (bottom left), 56 (bottom), 60 (middle left), 63, 64 (bottom), 68 (bottom), 71 (left), 73 (middle) – Corel Stock Photo Library: cover (insert), page 3 (top), 4 (bottom), 6 (bottom), 9 (top), 14 (top left), 18 (right) (top left), 22 (top right), 23 (top), 26 (background) (top left), 27 (top left) (bottom right) (bottom left), 29 (bottom right), 39 (bottom right) (right), 40 (top left) (background) (2nd from top right), 41, 45 (bottom), 50 (top) (bottom right), 51 (middle), 54 (top right), 67 (top right), 71 (background), 72 , 73 (background) – Deutsche Presseagentur GmbH, München: page 48 (middle right) – Hermann Dörre, München: page 8, 10, 11, 12, 14, 19, 20, 22, 23, 32, 33, 34, 36, 43, 44, 58, 62, 66, 67, 80 -Mary Evans Picture Library, London: page 72 (top left) – Exclusive Card Co., Edinburgh: page 17 (left) – Gallo Images, Parklands: page 48 (top left) – Christina Hackenberg, München: page 10 (2nd from top right) – Hong Kong Tourist Association: page 7 (bottom), 8 (bottom), 53 (bottom right) (background), 54 (top), 55, 56 (top right), 58 (top right) (top left), 59, 60 (top) 60 (bottom), 62 (left) (top right), 63 (left), 64 (top), 66 (top left), 67 (bottom left) – Lynda Hübner, München: page 34 (top) – IFA Bilderteam GmbH, München: page 31 (background), 65 (bottom) – ILTS International Language Teaching Services Pty Ltd, Essex: page 38 (bottom) – Schmidt/images.de: page 11 (2) – Interfoto Pressebild-Agentur Bildarchiv, München: page 73 (top) – Jamaica Tourist Board: page 70 (background) – Wolfgang Kleinbach, Kiel: page 58 (middle left) – Tina Klippel, Gröbenzell: page 22 (top left) – Matthias Kulka, Düsseldorf: cover (insert), page 3 (middle) – Bettina Lindenberg, München: page 25 (top left), 33 (top), 35, 42, 44 (top right), 76, 78 – Look GmbH, München: page 56 (left) – Uwe Mäder, Haimhausen: page 25 (top right) – Mercat Tours, Edinburgh: page 15 (bottom right) – Ursel Murray, Egelsbach: page 18 (background), 19 (top) – PA Photos Ltd., London: page 37 (top) – Picture Press/Life/Wrba, Hamburg: page 36 (background), 39 (bottom left) – reproduced with permission of Punch Ltd., London: page 39 (top) – Reuters NewMedia Inc.: page 72 (bottom left) – Claudia Schwarz, München: page 4 (top), 6 (top), 7 (background) (middle right), 10 (top right), 11 (1), 15 (top), 17 (bottom), 31 (middle), 32 (left) (right), 36 (top left), 37 (bottom), 38 (top), 44 (top left) (background), 45 (left), 46 (top) (bottom right), 47 (top) (bottom), 50 , 51 (background) (top right) (bottom right) – Mark Skinner Image Library: page 48 , 49 (background) – South African Tourism, Frankfurt: page 5, 49 (top), 50 (bottom left) – Still Moving picture company, Edinburgh: page 13 (bottom), 18 (bottom left), 24 (top) – Superbild Bildarchiv Erich Bach, Grünwald: page 68 (top), 71 (middle) – Chris Tyler, Isle of Skye: page 25 (bottom) – Vario-Press Photoagentur, Bonn: page 57 (bottom) – Bill Wassman: page 71 (bottom right) – Neil Wilson Publishing, Glasgow: page 13 (top), 20 (top right) – Sabine Wittmann, München: page 50 (middle left) – Zefa Zentrale Farbbild Agentur GmbH, Düsseldorf: cover, page 26 (top right)

We should be grateful for any information which might assist us in tracing the copyright owners of sources which we have been unable to acknowledge.